Teaching Reading Comprehension

ALISON DAVIS

THOMSON

NELSON

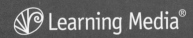

Learning Media®

Acknowledgments

The author wishes to thank the following people for their help, advice, and support:

Sue Brown, editor of the Teaching Reading Comprehension

Stuart McNaughton, the series editor of the Effective Teaching series, and Lois Thompson, author of the companion text on teaching writing, and reviewers Kathleen Doyle, Evelyn Maksimovitch, Janice Moore, Keith Hole, and Sharon Straathof for invaluable advice and reviews

The many teachers and colleagues with whom I have been lucky enough to work with, talk with, and learn with, in particular, those at Learning Media Limited and those involved in the PEN project in North Waikato, New Zealand.

For giving permission to quote their material, thanks to: T. S. Eliot; M. Pressley; P. Black; C. Snow, P. Griffin, and M. Burns; K. Hesse; J. Bonallack; T. Rasinski; T. Trabasso and E. Bouchard; Learning Media Limited; The Guilford Press; Faber & Faber; NFER-Nelson; John Wiley & Sons, Inc; Scholastic, Inc; Thomson Nelson; ASCD

Note: Learning Media has made every reasonable attempt to contact all holders of copyright for material quoted or adapted in this book. We would be pleased to hear from any copyright holders whom we have been unable to contact.

Foreword
by Joan Irwin

Reading assessment and instruction are topics of major concern to classroom teachers, literacy specialists, and school administrators. Improving student achievement and overcoming the achievement gap are central issues in discussions that educators and policy makers have about practices in reading instruction. In addition to concerns about assessment results and the utility of various assessment tools, teachers are called on to provide research-based instructional practices. Consequently, many professional development programs now focus on how to address the interrelationships between assessment and instruction and what teachers can do to enable students to become effective readers.

Alison Davis in this book, *Teaching Reading Comprehension*, brings a unique perspective to this important topic. She provides a research-based framework that clearly illustrates what it means to use data to inform instruction. Metacognitive comprehension instruction is the term Davis uses for this framework, which combines the principles of formative assessment with the components of metacognition in teaching reading. Within this framework, the author provides an array of examples that explicitly demonstrate what it means to teach reading in ways that enable students to acquire and apply a repertoire of strategies. Written from a teacher's perspective, these examples show the interrelationships and interdependencies among strategies for comprehension, word recognition, vocabulary, and fluency. The unique needs of both able learners and those who struggle with reading are integral to the discussions of strategies throughout the book. Davis presents a persuasive message that metacognitive comprehension instruction requires focus and persistence on the part of teachers working with all students in all areas of the curriculum.

Teaching Reading Comprehension is a book that invites the reader to reflect on what it means to be a teacher of readers. Davis acknowledges that there is no quick fix for effective reading instruction. Her message is perhaps best captured by this quotation:

> *"We had the experience but missed the meaning.*
> *And approach to the meaning restores the experience*
> *In a different form ..."*

T. S. Eliot, "The Dry Salvages," 1944
Lines 93–95

Contents

The teachers' CD-ROM that accompanies this book contains reproducible items for school and classroom use. These are indicated with an icon in the text.

From the author ...

When I first began teaching, I specialized in literacy education because I was fascinated with the process of learning to read, and more specifically, why some students find reading more difficult than others. As I taught across a range of grades, I saw that many teachers were particularly confused about reading comprehension and how they could best teach the strategies needed to develop this. In my professional development workshops, I heard comments that disturbed me:

> *"Reading comprehension strategies? I'm not sure how to teach them. I'm not sure I understand them myself."*

> *"I don't really teach them [comprehension strategies], but I'd like to."*

> *"I'm confused about what I should be teaching. Where does comprehension fit in with phonics?"*

Responses like these took me back to university in search of answers. As I devoured all the relevant research, I worked closely with teachers to try to find ways to help them use research insights to strengthen their teaching. I became particularly interested in what teachers were doing (or not doing!) with the assessment information they gathered about their students. It became clear to me that the most effective instruction was happening in the classrooms of teachers who understood how to teach comprehension (along with decoding, vocabulary, and fluency) and who based their teaching on the needs of the students. It was the use of both these strands that made the difference.

I incorporated this observation into the first year of my doctoral research and the results were startling. The grade 3 to 8 students whose teachers matched instruction to their needs and who were actively involved in the process of learning made much more progress than those in the control group. When teachers used a metacognitive approach to comprehension instruction, the students' learning raced ahead.

Over the next four years of the research project, the results consistently showed a dramatic increase in achievement. This happened across a wide range of schools, teachers, and students. It was clear that what the teachers of readers were doing made the difference. They learned to use a metacognitive approach to comprehension instruction, and they consistently engaged students in evaluating their own learning. They showed that they were able to take research into their daily practice and make a significant difference to the outcomes for their students.

In my work with teachers and students in many different schools and countries (including Canada, Singapore, and the United States), I'm constantly reminded of the critical role that teachers play in supporting their students to become confident and motivated comprehenders of text. That's why I've written this book. I wanted to share the lessons that I've learned so that others can deal with the complexities of teaching and learning to comprehend with ease and confidence.

I hope you find the ideas challenging, thought-provoking, and most of all, helpful in supporting you to raise your students' reading comprehension achievement.

We are learning to make
summary by identifying the
main ideas in each chapter.

We will be successful when

· we can write the main ideas for
  each chapter in our own words

· we can put these together and
  they make sense as a summary
  of the book.

Metacognitive Comprehension Instruction

Research has demonstrated that comprehension is a metacognitive behavior that can be taught in a way that brings together all the components of reading (word-recognition/decoding, vocabulary, fluency, and comprehension strategy use). Appendix 1.1 on page 32 summarizes the author's research.

When teachers combine a metacognitive approach with the principles of formative assessment, the result is metacognitive comprehension instruction. This book brings together these two important and influential bodies of research to show how the decisions made by the teacher impact on student achievement in reading comprehension.

This chapter describes the theoretical and research background to metacognitive comprehension instruction and outlines its application for teaching reading comprehension.

Key messages for teachers

- Research has an important role in informing and developing teaching practice.
- Effective comprehenders are metacognitively active as they read.
- Metacognition can be developed through instruction.
- Formative assessment helps teachers to be responsive to the specific needs of students.
- Metacognitive comprehension instruction draws together practice and research in metacognition and formative assessment.

Research and reading instruction

The goal of all teachers of reading is to develop readers who can understand and make use of what they read and who are motivated to read widely.

Good readers are metacognitive: they are aware of what they are doing as they read, and they can control their reading behavior to overcome problems. Researchers (Duffy, Roehler, and others from 1984; Pressley and others from 1991) have offered valuable insights that are based on the direct explanation of comprehension strategies to students. A central feature of Duffy and Roehler's (1989) direct explanation model was "mental modeling," where teachers think aloud to show students a comprehension strategy and how to use it. Several years later, Pressley coined the term "transactional strategies instruction" (TSI) to convey the idea that this kind of instruction also involves a complex network of transactions – between the student and the text, the student and the teacher, and students with students (see page 24). As teachers and students interact with texts and with one another, "transactions" take place among the participants and the text, resulting in the making of meaning. In transactional strategies instruction, meaning is determined by more than one person as students learn how to become strategic in their reading.

> *Transactional strategies instruction is all about teaching students to choose active reading over passive reading and to decide for themselves which strategic processes to use when they confront challenging texts.*
>
> Pressley, 2006, page 320

Within a similar timeframe, other research has focused on the use of formative assessment principles.

> … *"assessment" refers to all those activities undertaken by teachers* and by their students in assessing themselves, *which provide information to be used as feedback to modify the teaching and learning activities in which they are engaged.* Such assessment becomes "formative assessment" when the evidence is actually used to adapt the teaching work to meet the needs.
>
> Black and Wiliam, 1998, page 2

Teachers who use formative assessment know what to look for when they teach, they know how to interpret what they see and hear, how to respond to the students, and how to adjust their teaching. There is evidence that teaching using formative assessment principles is highly metacognitive and that assessment for formative purposes is central to learning with understanding (see page 18).

This book integrates the research on metacognition and formative assessment with the components of reading (word solving/phonemic awareness/phonics; vocabulary knowledge; fluency instruction and practice; comprehension) to show how comprehension is dependent on readers being aware of what they are doing as they use strategies to comprehend. Teachers who are intentional and knowledgeable hold the keys to truly effective comprehension instruction.

The nature of reading comprehension

Reading comprehension is a continuous and recurring process that builds up as readers engage with text. The more we read, the more knowledge and experience we take to the next text. A reader's knowledge and experience potentially includes everything he or she has done, felt, heard, seen, and read throughout life as well as the knowledge and experience about how the written language works. Good readers draw on this rich store in several different ways.

There is a great deal of research (Allington, 2001; Braunger and Lewis, 1998, 2006; Clay, 1991; Duffy, 2003; National Reading Panel, 2000; Pressley, 2001a, 2002a, 2002b, 2006) available to help teachers identify what effective comprehenders do. Good readers are active as they read. They draw on their knowledge of letter–sound relationships to decode words and develop word-recognition skills. They build vocabulary knowledge, and they learn to use a number of comprehension strategies. They develop patterned knowledge (such as the patterns found in different text genres, sentence forms, and spelling patterns) that allows new patterns to be detected almost automatically. In doing these things, good readers learn to monitor and adjust their use of reading strategies to assist them to gain meaning. They can use strategies and processes in an orchestrated way and can "shift gears" as they detect changes and challenges in texts.

Decoding, the act of solving unknown words using knowledge of letter or sound relationships, word patterns, and sight word recognition, is a skill that all students need to acquire to be successful readers. Good readers recognize many words on sight, but they can also figure out how to read words they have never seen before. This is because they are able to associate letters with sounds and blend the sounds to pronounce a

word. They are also able to make analogies with words or parts of words they already know. Comprehension requires more than accurate decoding, it also requires word-recognition fluency. If the reader has to put undue time and attention into decoding, overall meaning may be lost. For this reason, instruction needs to have an emphasis on the fluency as well as the accuracy of decoding. Explicit instruction that is integrated with context and linked to a student's prior knowledge will help students to decode and recognize unknown words quickly and easily. *See chapter 2 for further information about working out words.*

There is a clear association between readers' core vocabulary knowledge and their comprehension skills. Students build a wide vocabulary through repeated exposure and through instruction that develops their strategies for figuring out the meanings of words (for example, by using context, by using the meanings of root words, prefixes, suffixes, by considering synonyms and antonyms, and by looking for definitions in the text). *See chapter 3 for further information about vocabulary instruction.*

Good comprehenders learn to read fluently, during "in the head" silent reading and reading aloud. Reading fluently means being able to process text efficiently (without undue effort) and with comprehension. Fluent readers are able to control and monitor the pace of their reading, adjusting when they do not fully understand something. They are also alert to intonation and phrasing, and they draw on accurate and automatic word-recognition skills. *See chapter 4 for further information about reading fluency.*

Good reading is more than the sum of these parts. Research suggests that up to thirty cognitive and metacognitive processes are involved in comprehension (Block and Pressley, 2002). Readers learn to make use of a large number of comprehension strategies. These strategies can be likened to tools that readers use to access and develop meaning. The key strategies (described in this book) are making connections to prior knowledge, prediction and reprediction, visualizing, inferring, self-questioning, seeking clarification, summarizing, finding the main idea, analyzing and synthesizing, and evaluating. *See chapter 5 for further information about teaching comprehension strategies.*

Readers draw on these strategies before, during, and after reading. Sometimes the strategies are used consciously while at other times they are used without the reader's conscious attention. Good comprehenders use strategies as and when they are needed. This means that when a reader is having difficulty comprehending a text, the reader will use one or more strategies in rapid succession. This behavior is called self-monitoring: the reader knows whether he or she is comprehending, determines whether understanding was easy or difficult and why, and uses comprehension strategies to solve problems. Readers self-evaluate what they know and take appropriate steps to fix comprehension difficulties when they occur.

Metacognitive comprehension instruction

Metacognition is the term used by educators and researchers to describe the knowledge and awareness that a person has of his or her cognitive resources. Metacognition is thinking about thinking.

Metacognition is about readers "knowing" – knowing when they know, knowing when they don't know, and knowing what to do when they don't know.

In this book, metacognitive comprehension instruction includes all the elements that influence comprehension, including recognizing words, vocabulary, fluency, and comprehension strategies.

Metacognitive comprehension instruction describes the combination of research-based instructional practices with theoretical knowledge about teaching and learning.

Metacognitive comprehension instruction involves many factors that operate in combination with one another. They are each important in their own right and are not necessarily subsumed under one heading or another.

Metacognitive comprehension instruction involves:

- metacognition, prior knowledge, and schema theory
- formative assessment
- transactional strategies instruction (including the think-aloud approach)
- group teaching approaches
- talking about learning
- motivation and engagement.

Each factor is outlined in this chapter, and the examples and descriptions provided in further chapters show how teachers can provide powerful, effective comprehension instruction. This is not a quick fix: this kind of instruction requires focus, patience, and a willingness to pay attention to what students are actually doing as they read.

Metacognitive Comprehension Instruction

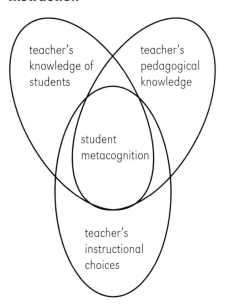

teacher's knowledge of students

teacher's pedagogical knowledge

student metacognition

teacher's instructional choices

When teachers combine what they know about their students with their knowledge of best practices to make informed instructional decisions, the resulting instruction will be metacognitively rich – it will encourage the development of students who are metacognitively aware. These are the students who are most likely to make significant gains in reading comprehension achievement.

Metacognition and the importance of prior knowledge

As readers learn to monitor their reading, they also learn what they can do to solve any problems they encounter. Effective readers use multiple strategies to assist their comprehension. They often do so subconsciously until they come to something they can't comprehend. It is at this point that metacognitively active readers deliberately draw on their strategies to support their reading and remove barriers to comprehension.

Metacognition can be developed through instruction. Research by Duffy and Roehler (1989) led to the development of the direct-explanation model and resulted in improved reading achievement. Students learned to use comprehension strategies in a highly metacognitive manner and were able to transfer their learning in new situations. Direct explanation is aimed at assisting students to consciously recognize problems and consciously reach solutions to them.

Further research (Braunger and Lewis, 2006; Pressley, 2001a, 2002a, 2002b, 2006; National Reading Panel, 2001) provided powerful evidence that most readers benefit enormously when lessons make the comprehension processes visible. Instructional approaches that enable students to learn about learning and to think about thinking are metacognitively rich: they deliberately assist students to take control of their learning. As students extend their knowledge, they become increasingly able to use what they have learned automatically. A key factor in this kind of instruction is recognition of the role played by the students' prior knowledge.

Prior knowledge and schema theory

Over many years, cognitive research (Ausubel, 1963; Forrest-Pressley and Waller, 1984; Garner, 1987) has shown how learning becomes a process of making meaning from unfamiliar events in the light of familiar ideas or experiences. Early work by Ausubel (1963) proposed that old information in memory can provide scaffolding for new information in text. Learners construct knowledge as they build "cognitive maps" for organizing and interpreting new information and concepts. Anderson and Pearson (1984) developed the theory that described "maps" or frameworks that are stored in memory as schema and explained the important role that schema play in interpreting new information.

The background knowledge that forms schema is gained through a lifetime of experiences (first hand and otherwise).

> *This rather amorphous background knowledge figures at the start of comprehension when the reader or listener's mental model fills in gaps to make sense of the information provided by speakers and writers. It appears again as the outcome of comprehension, carried forward as updated background knowledge ready for new experiences of listening or reading.*
>
> Snow, Griffin, and Burns; 2005; page 23

In the context of reading comprehension, prior knowledge is built up and changed over time as readers engage with text. Readers will, for example, have schema about a topic, an author, a text type, or a context, and they draw on this to build comprehension as they read. Their active participation in using and modifying their prior knowledge means that there is a very strong reciprocal relationship between prior knowledge and comprehension.

Instruction that aims to develop metacognition builds from and extends students' schema. The more students know about a topic, the more they can comprehend a text about the topic. Similarly, the more students comprehend, the more they will know. Learning is a process of making meaning out of new or unfamiliar events or ideas in light of familiar ideas or experiences.

As researchers argue (Fielding and Pearson, 1994), the relationship between prior knowledge and reading comprehension is essentially a reciprocal one. The relationship has two parts:

- developing students' knowledge base before reading
- building students' knowledge from the text during reading.

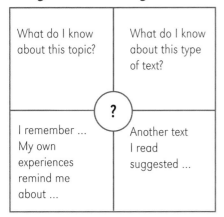

Using Prior Knowledge

What do I know about this topic?	What do I know about this type of text?
I remember ... My own experiences remind me about ...	Another text I read suggested ...

Understanding this relationship is important as teachers plan their reading comprehension instruction to make deliberate links to their students' prior knowledge and to support students to make links themselves. Using and building on students' prior knowledge as a springboard to enhancing comprehension will include linking to the students':

- knowledge related to the content of the text
- knowledge about the textual similarities and differences in various genres and subject areas
- social and personal knowledge
- cultural knowledge and experiences
- knowledge of the author, for example, the author's style, position, and purpose for writing.

Formative assessment

Formative assessment is not testing. It is an ongoing, recursive process through which students become active in their learning by thinking and talking about what they can do as readers and about their comprehension strengths and needs. In this respect, formative assessment supports a metacognitive approach to teaching and learning.

Formative assessment also gives teachers explicit information about the learning needs of a student, or a group of students, in the course of an instructional program. In order to do this, formative assessment is integrated with instruction to improve the learning and achievement of students. When used effectively by teachers, formative assessment has been proven to produce significant and often substantial learning gains (Black and Wiliam, 2001; Clarke, 2001, 2005).

Formative assessment procedures involve a number of strategies to identify student needs and to plan for goal-focused instruction.

Formative Assessment Procedures

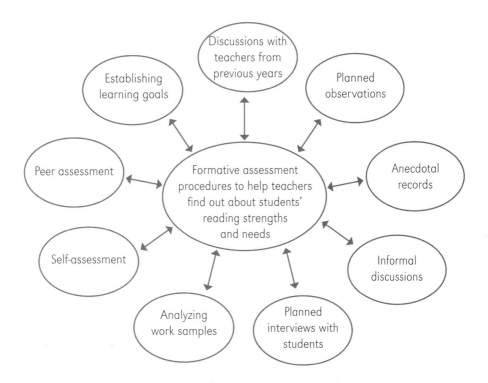

Identifying students' changing needs
Discussions with teachers from previous years

Students' previous teachers are important sources of information.
Teachers can discuss the achievements, abilities, strengths, and needs
of individual students. This information, which may be verbal or
written, can help to determine trends in progress, insights into areas of
difficulty, and the results of any interventions. Other professionals who
have provided additional assistance will also have valuable information
to share. Teachers need to be aware that some of this information
may include opinions rather than facts and that students will respond
differently in different settings.

Planned observations

Using planned observations, teachers observe students at work, looking for behaviors that indicate comprehension and metacognition: an understanding of what they are learning, how they are learning, and why they are learning. The behaviors are usually predetermined and arise from "hunches" teachers have as a result of previous lessons, from marked work, and from informal discussions and observations. Planned observations provide a means of monitoring lesson goals, determining whether students learned what the teacher planned, examining student participation, and identifying the next learning priorities.

Anecdotal records

Teachers make notes about students, usually arising from a planned observation, a discussion with a student, a student goal-setting session, or from marking and analyzing student work. The notes record what a student is learning, what he or she finds hard, what has been learned, and what the next priorities will be.

Informal discussions

These are planned opportunities for students to talk with their teacher and with peers about their learning, their understanding of text, and their comprehension. Through informal discussions, students are able to focus on their understanding, and teachers are able to talk about the process of learning, gathering information on strengths and needs that will inform future learning goals and instructional decisions.

Planned interviews with students

In these more formal discussions, the teacher meets with a student, or group of students, with a set goal in mind. The goal is planned to enable the teacher to learn about the comprehension strategies the students use, their attitudes towards reading, and how they view themselves as a comprehenders.

Analyzing work samples

The teacher and the students analyze work samples (completed graphic organizers, diagrams or charts, short answer paragraphs) in relation to shared learning goals and success criteria. This analysis informs future teaching priorities.

When teachers analyze student behavior as they read, discuss, and respond to texts, they gain valuable information to inform their instructional decisions – decisions about the strategies students need to learn or practice, about what teaching approach to use, about how much time to spend, and about how to plan for follow-up and maintenance opportunities. Analysis allows teachers to ask questions such as the following:

- What does this task ask the students to do? What parts of this can the students do independently? With guidance?
- What has the student been able to do in the past?
- What kinds of errors have been made? How often are they made?
- What skills or understandings are underlying these errors?
- Does this match with other information I have about this student's learning needs?

And after considering this …

- What feedback do I give the student?
- How do we set learning goals?
- What is the best way for this student to learn this?
- What does this mean for the instruction I plan and the kinds of instructional activities I offer?

Peer and self-assessment

Peer assessment involves students assessing their learning with a peer in relation to shared learning goals, providing one another with feedback on their work and talking about the process of learning. Lesson goals and success criteria are important in guiding peer assessment.

Self-assessment involves students reflecting on whether they have achieved the learning goals. Students will refer to the goals and success criteria to direct their self-assessment.

Teachers can provide metacognitive instruction (explaining, modeling, and guided practice) to help students understand how to assess their own and one another's work by using agreed-on success criteria. This enables strong and focused discussion on learning between the students. When teachers and students subsequently discuss these assessments together, the talk about learning will lead to future goal setting and will inform instruction. Students will initially need frequent reminders that the assessment relates to the agreed criteria, not to the individual.

Goal-focused instruction

Establishing learning goals and success criteria

Learning goals are the key goals for a lesson. They are established from curriculum goals tailored to the priorities identified for students based on assessment. They are informed by observation, anecdotal notes, informal discussion, interviews with students, student self-assessment, goal setting, and analysis of work samples. Learning goals may be content or strategy related, or a combination of both.

Success criteria are the measures that show whether the students have achieved the learning goals. The students write them with the teacher's support, and they answer the question, "How will we know we've learned this?" They are simple, specific statements that relate directly to the goal and the text or task. They are not to be confused with task instructions – they are about what the students *learn.*

Using formative assessment

Formative assessment allows teachers to build reading comprehension instruction around the interests, strengths, and needs of their students. Formative assessment has a central role in deciding instructional content, the selection of text, the pace of a lesson, and the teaching approach. By applying a combination of the procedures listed above, teachers of readers come to learn more about the comprehension needs of their students and are more able to match student need and instruction.

Involving students in formative assessment involves them in their own learning, and this has direct links to cognition and metacognition. Learning is enhanced through sharing learning goals at the start of each lesson. Together, teachers and students talk about the intended learning and what the students will be able to do if they have achieved the learning goal (the success criteria).

The most important benefit of formative assessment is that it focuses the student and the teacher on the goal, the purpose for which it was set, and the learning benefits from achieving it.

This procedure is referred to as sharing learning goals (also referred to as learning intentions or lesson objectives). Teachers typically select one goal for a lesson. By recording this in writing, students and teacher can refer to it as the lesson progresses to see how learning is developing. The teacher may also ask the students to think about what they expect to learn as a result of the lesson and the goal. Together, students and teacher can write one or more criteria to determine whether the goal has been attained.

If difficulties are discovered during the lesson, instruction can be adjusted. At the conclusion of the lesson, the students and the teacher can refer back to the goal to monitor their progress. If they wrote success criteria, they can discuss whether they were met. As a result of these discussions, the teacher and students can set goals and related success criteria for subsequent lessons.

Sharing of goals and success criteria

Rosanne identified through her data that a group of students needed support with summarizing. She decided to focus her teaching on learning to use the summarizing strategy. The overall learning goal for the students was:

We are learning to summarize.

She chose to focus on identifying the main idea inside each paragraph of a report as one aspect of summarizing. The first learning goal for this block of work was:

We are learning to identify the key idea in each paragraph to help us to summarize.

Rosanne shared the goal with the group, and they discussed what they would be able to do by achieving the goal. From this discussion, they wrote the success criteria for the lesson:

We will be successful when we can:

> identify the key ideas in the paragraph
> justify to each other why we think they are key ideas
> pick out the key sentence/ key words
> give a one sentence summary of the main idea in this paragraph.

Transactional strategies instruction (TSI)

The importance of instruction that develops metacognition has been supported by research to identify the features of effective comprehension instruction. As discussed earlier in this chapter, one instructional approach that arose from this research was that of transactional strategies instruction (TSI), a term coined by Pressley and his colleagues (Pressley, 2001a, 2002a, 2002b, 2006; Pressley and Brainerd, 1985; Pressley and Woloshyn, 1995; Schneider and Pressley, 1989) to describe a way of teaching that promotes interactions between teacher, students, and texts to develop the students' ability to actively comprehend, to remember what they have read, and to be able to talk about their interpretations of texts.

TSI involves the teacher and students in learning about comprehension strategies together. It is a long-term approach, is highly metacognitive, and it involves a number of principles that are central to any pedagogy that aims to bring about learning with understanding. Together with formative assessment, the pedagogical principles of TSI form the framework for metacognitive comprehension instruction.

Principles of transactional strategies instruction

- Teachers provide students with a direct explanation of the focus strategy. This explanation includes telling students what the strategy is, how it assists reading comprehension, and what readers do when they use the strategy.
- Teachers model the strategy to the class or small group. This is frequently done by using the think-aloud approach (see next page). By doing this, teachers provide information on how and when to use the strategy.
- Teachers share information on the learning benefits that can be gained from the use of the strategy.
- Classroom instruction provides opportunities for collaborative, guided, paired, and independent use of the strategy.
- Classroom instruction provides opportunities for students to model and explain the use of the strategy to one another.
- Classroom instruction provides opportunities for students to use the strategies on their own and monitor their use.
- Students are provided with ongoing opportunities to use this strategy in conjunction with others.

The think-aloud approach

The think-aloud approach (Brown and Lyttle, 1988) involves the readers in thinking out loud (verbalizing) the processes, thoughts, and ideas that they are engaging in as they read. It is a central part of TSI. Teachers can think aloud to model a process (for example, the application of a decoding or comprehension strategy) and to show students how to verbalize their thoughts. With support and practice, students can use the think-aloud approach to verbalize, not only the information and ideas, but also the internal thought processes that they are engaged in as they make meaning. When students verbalize their thoughts in this way, they make their thought processes accessible to others. This in turn, allows for discussion and feedback between students and between students and their teachers on the process of learning how to make meaning.

The think-aloud approach is used to support student reading comprehension in the following ways:

- Teachers think aloud to make the strategies they are using explicit as they read to their students.
- Teachers think aloud to describe how they combine their prior knowledge with the ideas and content in the text to develop meaning.
- Students think aloud to explain their thought processes to the teacher as they work their way through a text.
- Students think aloud to explain their thought processes to their peers as they work their way through a text.

By thinking aloud, students make their learning (the processes they go through and the strategies they use) visible to themself and to others. It is an effective way for students to understand what and how they are learning and the benefits they are gaining as a result.

Group teaching approaches

To be effective, instruction needs to focus on students' needs. Students' needs vary widely and change frequently. For these reasons, and because of the central role of discussion and collaboration, small-group approaches are most effective for teaching students how to become skilled comprehenders. There are several group-based approaches that can be used to teach reading comprehension effectively. They include shared reading, guided reading, and reciprocal reading, and they are all appropriate for metacognitive comprehension instruction for students in grades 3 to 8. Each approach provides a means for direct and explicit instruction that includes:

- sharing learning goals and success criteria with students
- providing opportunities for student self-assessment and feedback from peers and teachers
- teaching and learning specific comprehension strategies
- demonstrating how these strategies can be used together to make and explore meaning from text
- making the thinking skills transparent as the students comprehend text through modeling, explaining, telling, and deliberately sharing their thinking – the think-aloud strategy
- providing encouragement and support for students to become active when they process text
- focusing on developing the co-ordinated and independent use of a variety of comprehension strategies.

The teaching approaches should engage students in talking about the text as well as their learning and their developing understanding of what it means to be a good comprehender. Students who are able to think and talk about the strategies they use are better able to draw on their own knowledge to solve problems as they encounter them.

Many teachers will be familiar with some or all of these approaches, but others may need to adjust their instructional practices, classroom organization, and management in order to use group teaching. As teachers modify their teaching to provide metacognitive comprehension instruction, they will also strengthen their implementation of shared, guided, and reciprocal reading. This includes goal setting at the beginning of each lesson, reflection on the goal during the lesson, use of teacher and student demonstration and explanation, and regular use of the think-aloud approach. This stronger focus on metacognitive

Name: Oska **Date:** 3/4/07

I am learning to:
use what I know about the meanings of prefixes, suffixes, and root words to figure out tricky words

What I did:
multicultural = multi / cultur / al = relating to many cultures

extraordinary = extra / ordinary = out of the ordinary, very unusual

antidote = anti / dote = against a poison

anthropology = anthro / pology = study of people

comprehension instruction will in turn lead to improved reading comprehension achievement for their students. *See chapters 6 and 7 for descriptions and illustrations of these approaches and for information on how to organize for group instruction.*

Talking about learning

Talk can assist students to describe and monitor their comprehension, describe what they are doing when they comprehend, express their ideas, and reflect on their own thinking and learning. Furthermore, talk enables other students to learn from their peers' experiences and knowledge. Opportunities for talk-as-learning include talk between pairs, talk within a peer group, talk in small groups, and talk between the teacher and the student.

If students are not used to talking about their learning, it may be necessary to spend time teaching them how to share and justify their ideas, to give and receive feedback, and to learn the language of classroom discussions. There is a parallel need for teachers to develop an awareness of their own language use, which includes providing information, giving feedback, mediation, and modeling (Johnston, 2004; McNaughton, 2002; Villaume and Brabham, 2002).

Talking about learning is woven through every component of metacognitive comprehension instruction and, therefore, every part of this book. *See page 77 for an example of a conversation between a teacher and student.*

Motivation and engagement

Students who believe they are good at reading are generally motivated and have a positive feeling and commitment toward reading. There is considerable value in encouraging students to become good at reading, and to know what good readers actually do. There are a number of ways that classroom instruction can harness and foster student motivation. These include:

- appropriate text selection
- student involvement in selection of topics, authors, genres, and themes

- student knowledge and understanding of the lesson purpose
- allowing students to be actively engaged (through interactions) in the lesson
- providing a variety of follow-up activities
- alignment of follow-up activities with students' interests and abilities
- encouraging constructive two-way feedback within lessons.

When students have a sense of control over their learning, they are far more likely to be engaged and motivated in reading. Metacognitive comprehension instruction gives students this control over their own learning.

Summary

This book is about assisting teachers to develop approaches that enable students in grades 3 to 8 to take control of their learning and to foster their motivation and engagement toward reading. It's about drawing students' attention to the cognitive strategies that they can use to comprehend the texts they have to read, as well as the ones they choose to read. These strategies can be used consciously or instinctively, without the reader's conscious attention. The important thing is that students learn to understand strategies for comprehension and can control their use when they need them.

Metacognitive comprehension instruction can lead to significant, sustained gains in reading comprehension achievement for students. The approaches used enable students to learn about learning and to think about thinking – they are metacognitively rich. By showing students how to think about when, how, and why they use comprehension strategies, teachers are able to influence learning outcomes and make learning transparent.

This is achieved by providing deliberate and explicit instruction on the strategies employed by effective comprehenders. It means sharing the teaching and the learning with students – letting them in on the "secrets" so that they understand how their learning develops, what helps them to learn better, and how they can know whether they are being successful. A major benefit of this form of instruction is the development of engaged and motivated students.

References and recommended reading

Allington, R. (2000). *What Really Matters for Struggling Readers: Designing Research-based Programs*. New York, New York: Longman.

Anderson, R. C. and Pearson, P. D. (1984). "A Schema-theoretic View of Basic Processes in Reading". In *Handbook of Reading Research*, ed. P. D. Pearson. New York, New York: Longman, pp. 255–291.

Ausubel, D. P. (1963). *The Psychology of Meaningful Verbal Learning*. New York, New York: Grune and Stratton.

Black, P. and William, D. (1998). *Inside the Black Box: Raising Standards through Classroom Assessment*. London: King's College School of Education.

Block, C. C. and Pressley, M. (2001). *Comprehension Instruction: Research-based Best Practices*. New York: The Guilford Press.

Braunger, J. and Lewis, J. (1997). *Building a Knowledge Base in Reading*. Newark, Delaware: International Reading Association.

Braunger, J. and Lewis, J. P. (2006). (2nd ed.). *Building a Knowledge Base in Reading*. Newark, Delaware: International Reading Association.

Brown, C. S. and Lytle, S. L. (1988). "Merging Assessment and Instruction: Protocols in the Classroom". In *Re-examining Reading Diagnosis: New Trends and Procedures*, ed. S.M. Glazer, L.W. Searfoss, and L.M. Gentile. Newark, Delaware: International Reading Association, pp. 94–102.

Brown, R., Pressley, M., Van Meter, P., and Schuder, T. (1996). "A Quasi-experimental Validation of Transactional Strategies Instruction with Low-achieving Second-grade Readers". *Journal of Educational Psychology*, 88 (1), pp. 18–37.

Chappuis, J. (2005). "Helping Students Understand Assessment". *Educational Leadership*, 63(3), pp. 39–53.

Chappuis, S. and Stiggins, R. J. (2002). "Classroom Assessment for Learning". *Educational Leadership*, 60(1), pp. 40–43.

Clarke, S. (2001). "Closing the Gap through Formative Assessment: Effective Distance Marking in Elementary Schools in England". Paper presented at AERA Conference, New Orleans.

Clarke, S. (2005). *Formative Assessment in Action: Weaving the Elements Together*. London: Hodder Murray.

Clay, M. M. (1991). *Becoming Literate: The Construction of Inner Control*. Portsmouth, New Hampshire: Heinemann.

Dowhower, S. L. (1999). "Supporting a Strategic Stance in the Classroom: A Comprehension Framework for Helping Teachers Help Students to Be Strategic". *The Reading Teacher*, 52(7), pp. 672–683.

Duffy, G. G. (2003). *Explaining Reading: A Resource for Teaching Concepts, Skills, and Strategies*. New York, New York: The Guilford Press.

Duffy, G. C. and Roehler, L. R. (1989). "Why Strategy Instruction Is So Difficult and What We Need to Do about It." In *Cognitive Strategy Research: From Basic Research to Educational Applications*, ed. C. B. McCormick, G. Miller, and M. Pressley. New York: Springer-Verlag, pp. 133–154.

Earl, L. M. (2003). *Assessment As Learning: Using Classroom Assessment to Maximize Student Learning*. Thousand Oaks, California: Corwin Press.

Elley, W.B. (2001). *STAR: Supplementary Tests of Achievement in Reading for Years 4 to 9.* Wellington, New Zealand: New Zealand Council for Educational Research.

Elley, W.B. (2003). *STAR: Supplementary Tests of Achievement in Reading for Year 3.* Wellington, New Zealand: New Zealand Council for Educational Research.

Expert Panel on Literacy in Grades 4 to 6 in Ontario (2004). *Literacy for Learning: The Report of the Expert Panel on Literacy in Grades 4 to 6 in Ontario.* Ontario Ministry of Education.

Fielding, L. G. and Pearson, P. D. (1994). "Reading Comprehension: What Works?" *Educational Leadership*, 51(5), pp. 2–68.

Forrest-Pressley, D. and Waller, T. G. (1984). *Cognition, Metacognition, and Reading.* New York, New York: Springer-Verlag.

Garner, R. (1987). *Metacognition and Reading Comprehension.* Norwood, New Jersey: Ablex Publishing Corporation.

Glazer, S.M., Searfoss, L.W., and Gentile, L. N. (1988). ed. *Re-examining Reading Diagnosis: New Trends and Procedures.* Newark, Delaware: International Reading Association, pp. 94–102.

Guskey, T. R. (2003). "How Classroom Assessments Improve Learning". *Educational Leadership*, 60(5), pp. 6–11.

Johnston, P. H. (2004). *Choice Words: How Our Language Affects Children's Learning.* Portland, Maine: Stenhouse.

Keene, E. O. and Zimmerman, S. (1997). *Mosaic of Thought: Teaching Comprehension in a Reader's Workshop.* Portsmouth, New Hampshire: Heinemann.

McKenna, M. C. and Stahl, S. A. (2003). *Assessment for Reading Instruction.* New York, New York: The Guilford Press.

McNaughton, S. (2002). *Meeting of Minds.* Wellington, New Zealand: Learning Media.

Ministry of Education (2003). *Effective Literacy Practice in Years 1 to 4.* Wellington, New Zealand: Learning Media.

Ministry of Education (2006). *Effective Literacy Practice in Years 5 to 8.* Wellington, New Zealand: Learning Media.

National Reading Panel (2000). *Report of the National Reading Panel.* Washington DC: Government Printing Office. www.nationalreadingpanel.org

National Reading Panel (2001). *Teaching Children to Read: Report of the Comprehension Instruction Subgroup to the National Institute on Child Health and Development.* Washington, DC: National Academy Press.

Pressley, M. (2001a). "Comprehension Instruction: What Makes Sense Now, What Might Make Sense Soon". *Reading Online*, 5(2). www.readingonline.org/articles/handbook/pressley

Pressley, M. (2001b). *Effective Beginning Reading Instruction: A Paper Commissioned by the National Reading Conference.* Chicago, Illinois: National Reading Conference. www.nrconline.org/publications/pressleywhite2.pdf

Pressley, M. (2002a). "Comprehension Strategies Instruction". In *Comprehension Instruction: Research-based Best Practices*, ed. C. C. Block and M. Pressley. New York, New York: The Guilford Press, pp. 11–27.

Pressley, M. (2002b). *Reading Instruction That Works: The Case for Balanced Teaching* (2nd ed.). New York, New York: The Guilford Press.

Pressley, M. (2006). *Reading Instruction That Works: The Case for Balanced Teaching.* (3rd ed.). New York, New York: The Guilford Press.

Pressley, M. and Brainerd, C. J. (1985). *Cognitive Learning and Memory in Children: Progress in Cognitive Development Research*. New York, New York: Springer-Verlag.

Pressley, M. and Woloshyn, V. (1995). *Cognitive Strategy Instruction That Really Improves Children's Academic Performance*. Cambridge, Massachusetts: Brookline Books.

RAND Reading Study Group. (2001). *Reading for Understanding: Toward a Research and Development Program in Reading Comprehension*. Santa Monica, California: RAND Education.

Schneider, W. and Pressley, M. (1989). *Memory Development between 2 and 20*. New York, New York: Springer–Verlag

Smith, J. and Elley, W. (1997). *How Children Learn to Read*. Auckland, New Zealand: Longman.

Snow, C. E., Griffin, P., and Burns, M. S. ed. (2005). *Knowledge to Support the Teaching of Reading: Preparing Teachers for a Changing World*. San Francisco, California: Jossey-Bass.

Stiggins, R. (2006). "Assessment for Learning: A Key to Motivation and Achievement". *Edge*, 2(2). Phi Delta Kappa International. www.pdkintl.org

Villaume, S. K. and Brabham, E. G. (2002). "Comprehension Instruction: Beyond Strategies". *The Reading Teacher*, 55 (7), pp. 672–675.

Wiggins, G. (1990). "The Case for Authentic Assessment". *Practical Assessment, Research, and Evaluation*. http://PAREonline.net/getvn.asp?v = 2&n = 2

Research summary

The following brief summary of the author's research is provided as background to the work that underpins this book. A full research report will be available in 2008.

The author's recent four-year research involved working with teachers and literacy leaders in a cluster of thirteen schools. The aim was to explore the characteristics of teacher expertise associated with raising the reading comprehension of students. Although all students were included in the study, there was a parallel research focus on raising the comprehension achievement of low achieving students: every teacher was asked to identify and follow the progress of a small group of low achieving students in greater detail than usual.

Methodology

The first year of the study developed over three phases using an action–research methodology. At each phase, the author systematically observed, analyzed, and enhanced (through professional development) the expertise of the teachers in the study. The focus was on identifying and developing the instructional practices that were most likely to be associated with improvements in student reading comprehension. (See chapter 1 for a discussion of these practices.)

Three sources of data were gathered at each of these three phases to inform the action research:

1. Data from participating teachers through taped, transcribed, and coded interviews
2. Researcher in-class observation (videotaped and coded)
3. Student reading comprehension achievement assessment data, gathered through the Supplementary Test of Reading Comprehension (STAR, Elley, 2001, 2003).

Data gathered from the first phase indicated that a high proportion of students were underachieving in the areas of sentence comprehension, paragraph comprehension, and vocabulary. By contrast, their teachers believed they were doing a "good" job of teaching reading comprehension. The second and subsequent years of the study used this data to inform the direction of the research.

Measuring student achievement

Student reading comprehension achievement results were gathered using STAR on three occasions in the first year. The students were administered sub-tests to measure:

- word recognition
- sentence comprehension
- paragraph comprehension, and
- vocabulary range.

Students in grades 6 to 8 were also measured on their understanding of the language of advertising and of reading different styles of writing.

The STAR tool is designed for repeated measurement within and across years and provides a recognized, standardized, and norm-referenced measure of reading comprehension that can readily be compared across students and schools.

Stanines

Teachers use a table of stanine norms (refer Elley, 2001, p. 18) to convert a student's raw scores to a stanine score. Stanine scoring uses a 9-point scale (from 1 to 9) to indicate how well each student achieves on a test in relation to others in the same grade level at the same time of the year. Students who score at stanine 9 are in the top 4 percent of their year level nationwide, pupils who score stanine 5 are in the middle 20 percent nationwide, and pupils who score stanine 1 are in the lowest 4 percent nationwide.

Professional development

During the first year of the study, teachers within the cluster were invited to participate in professional development that focused on the analysis of student data to inform reading comprehension instruction. This included:

- the selection of appropriate teaching approaches, resources, and activities;
- teacher and student use of formative assessment practices;
- the importance of taking a strategic approach to comprehension teaching;
- the development of metacognitive comprehension instruction.
- In the first year of the study, participation in the many forms of professional development available with the author was optional.

In the second and subsequent years of the study, all teachers in the cluster participated in professional learning opportunities that included workshops, collaborative problem solving, teacher goal setting, buddy mentoring, and in-class observations and video taping. Cluster-wide grade level workshops focused on teaching approaches that targeted the reading comprehension needs of students. Student achievement data were used to inform the deliberate acts of teaching undertaken as teachers developed their knowledge and expertise in metacognitive comprehension instruction.

Results

At the end of the first year of the study, results showed that there were large differences in the reading comprehension achievement of those students taught by the teachers who had engaged in the professional development compared with those taught by teachers who chose not to participate. After twenty weeks of instruction from teachers who had modified their teaching, students' mean stanines had shifted from 4.32 (SD = 2.12) to 4.87 (SD = 2.25). This gain of 0.55 was a significant improvement.

By contrast, the students whose teachers had not participated in professional development made gains, but they were much smaller: the mean stanine moved from 4.03 (SD = 1.91) to 4.21 (SD = 2.58), a gain of 0.18. The students in the first group showed significantly greater gains ($t=2.03$, $p=<.05$).

The second and subsequent years of the study built on the professional development undertaken by the author with the teachers in the first year and focused on metacognitive comprehension instruction. This meant that all the teachers in the study from year two onwards were involved in professional development.

Gains in student reading comprehension continued to be evident. In the second year, the mean stanine for all students rose from 4.20 (SD = 2.05) to 4.82 (SD = 2.10). There was a 0.62 gain across all common students over this time making this a highly significant result ($t = 16.07$, $p < .01$). The increase in comprehension achievement continued into the third year where again there was a significant improvement in the mean stanine score for the total group. Over the period of the third year of instruction, the mean stanine score for students in the cluster rose from 4.51 (SD = 1.98) to 5.05 (SD = 1.98). This was a 0.54 gain across all common students in 2005 ($t = 16.54$, $p < .01$). These results were sustained into the fourth year.

In addition, the data indicated that in every year of the study, the gains were being achieved irrespective of gender and ethnicity. The changes that teachers were making to how they taught and what they taught resulted in achievement gains for all students.

Conclusions

Metacognitive comprehension instruction enabled the teachers to carry out reading instruction that also promoted word recognition strategies, vocabulary knowledge, fluency, and extensive reading of books.

Key factors in the gains for students were the teachers' commitment to their own professional learning and to modifying their practice in light of student data along with their increased understanding of reading comprehension. Despite changes of teachers and school leaders within the cluster, the reading comprehension achievement of all students was improved, and these improvements were sustained over time.

Working with Word Strategies

The purpose of this chapter is to draw teachers' attention to the importance of providing all students with strategies that they can follow when they encounter words they do not recognize. While most students in grades 3 to 8 will have already developed some strategies for figuring out words, many will require support with figuring out more complex words as they encounter more challenging texts across all areas of the curriculum. Teachers who are aware of word strategies and how they are used will be able to offer instruction when and where it is needed.

Key messages for teachers

- The ability to identify (recognize, decode, solve, figure out) words rapidly is integral to student success in learning how to comprehend written texts.

- Learning to recognize words includes having knowledge and skills in word attack (decoding, structural analysis), and basic sight words.

- Word recognition knowledge and skills include phonological, phonemic, orthographic, and morphological awareness.

- Students need to have strategies for using the context as well as the parts of the word itself to help figure out unfamiliar words.

- For some students beyond the early grades, a lack of knowledge and skills in one or more of these areas is a cause of underachievement in reading comprehension.

- All teachers have a responsibility to provide students with the knowledge and skills to know how words work.

- Instruction should be highly metacognitive to ensure that students know what word solving/decoding strategies they can employ, when to employ them, how to employ them, and how to monitor their own developing awareness and understanding.

- When students are actively involved in their own learning, they are more likely to develop metacognitive understandings about how words work.

When readers are not skilled at figuring out words quickly, comprehension is low. However, if students can read words quickly and automatically, then word recognition will not interfere with comprehension.

All students need a clear set of steps that they can understand and follow when they encounter words they do not recognize. There is growing acknowledgment that some degree of explicit phonics instruction is necessary beyond beginning reading and that this instruction is useful, not only in developing the reading capabilities of struggling readers, but also of average and above average readers (NICHD, 2000).

In grades 3 to 8, this instruction will focus on assisting students to decode and figure out longer words, particularly those that are made more complex by their structure and context (for example, multi-syllabic words, and subject-specific academic vocabulary). Such instruction is necessary as students encounter a growing variety of texts across the curriculum. This means that instruction in figuring out words should include mathematics, social studies, science, and other subjects, as well as literacy. Ideally, word study will be embedded within the context of all ongoing instruction.

Knowing how words work

There are two main approaches to teaching word recognition that are supported by research. These are:

1. teaching students to sound out words
2. teaching students to decode new words by analogy to words they already know.

Both of these approaches are complementary and should be included as students learn to become active comprehenders of text. The teaching and learning activities in this chapter build on these approaches.

Sounding out words

In order to teach students how to recognize unfamiliar words, teachers need a good knowledge of the sounds in the English language and the ways sounds are represented in written language.

There are twenty-six letters in the English alphabet, and each one represents particular sounds. Some of these letters represent the same sound all the time. Others represent different sounds depending on the letters around them, for example, the short and long vowel sounds. This means there can be more than one sound for some letters, with research indicating that there are between forty-three and forty-six different sounds in total.

When teachers make this knowledge explicit, they are supporting and developing students' ability to figure out words they do not know.

Decoding a word is not simply a matter of linking one letter to one sound, just as knowing the letter names alone is not enough for students to be able to decode.

Teachers who have a good understanding of the concepts related to word recognition will be better able to identify the learning needs of their students and to plan for their instruction. *See the glossary for explanations of the terms used about word recognition.*

Using analogy

Students can be taught to figure out many unknown words by finding and comparing parts of the word with words they already know. This is called using analogy. Students examine the unknown word looking for parts that are like another word. In its simplest form, a student who encounters *that* for the first time could figure it out by making analogies with known words *the* and *cat*. Analogies can be made with word families (using knowledge of onset and rime), with root/base words, or with other parts of words, such as prefixes and suffixes. For example:

- *delight, slight, plight* all contain the rime *-ight* that students may already know from *fight*
- *construction* contains the root word *construct*
- *speciality* contains the root word *special*.

Teaching students to verbalize the strategies they use will help them to consolidate both the new word and the process used for figuring it out.

Teachers need to have a sound knowledge of how words work. *See chapter 3 for further information about the ways that word meanings relate to root words, derivations, and affixes.* Knowledge about these features contributes greatly to students' word recognition knowledge and skills, as well as to their understanding of vocabulary.

Identifying student needs

As discussed in chapter 1, teachers collect data about the strengths and needs of their students before they decide what to teach. They can do this by using a variety of word recognition assessment tools (such as letter–sound tests, blend tests, pseudo word tests) and through ongoing formative assessment (observation, questioning, discussion, marking work, collaboratively setting learning goals and success criteria, giving feedback). The data they gather and analyze will also help them to determine the best way of teaching the knowledge and skills that their students need.

Teaching includes both direct and follow-up support the students receive through independent and group activities. This means that instruction (teacher and student directed) occurs both within and outside planned lessons.

The following three examples of formative assessments show how teachers can collect data to identify their students' word recognition abilities and needs during the normal course of a day.

Targeted observations

These observations can be carried out during a shared or guided reading lesson. The teacher determines the target (specific focus) for the observation and decides how to carry it out. Some possible observation options and reasons for using them are shown in the following table.

Reading observation options	Benefits
Teacher observes a student in a one-to-one situation reading aloud a familiar (known) text.	Provides opportunity to see how much the student understands when there is prior knowledge of content
Teacher observes a student in a one-to-one situation reading aloud an unfamiliar text.	Provides insight into strategies a student can draw on when there is no prior knowledge of content Provides insight of strategy use in an unfamiliar context
Teacher observes a student or a group of students reading aloud and/or independently during their classroom reading instruction.	Provides opportunities to observe in a natural instructional setting and explore how student/s interact with text and text challenges
Teacher observes a student or a group of students during their independent reading time.	Provides opportunities to observe how students transfer learned reading behaviors from instruction to independent reading
Teacher observes a student or a group of students during cross-curricula reading opportunities throughout the day.	Provides opportunities to determine whether the students exhibit the same behaviors in different contexts

Targeted observations could follow these steps:

1. Determine the target word-recognition skills and behaviors.

2. Make decisions about the best options for the observations.

3. Select an appropriate text that will assist the observations, for example, a text chosen for instruction.

4. Develop a way of recording the observations, for example, a checklist or a space for making brief notes.

5. Introduce the text and provide a summary to enable the students to activate prior knowledge.

6. Listen to the students read (or observe their silent reading) and make notes on their reading behaviors.

7. Discuss the results with the students and together decide on suitable learning goals (see page 22).

Recording of observations may be based around these kinds of questions:

- How does the student approach an unknown word when reading a text for the first time? Does this vary between a seen and unseen text? If so how?

- What part of an unknown word does the student find difficult to solve?

- Does this relate to the students' knowledge of prefixes, suffixes, two-letter blends, three-letter blends, digraphs, or other features?

- Is the student able to articulate difficulty? Can the student offer suggestions of what could be done when encountering unknown words?

- Is the student able to independently draw on strategies when encountering unknown words?

- What strategies does the student draw on? (For example, knowledge of letter–sound combinations; making links between which letters and letter patterns make sounds; knowledge of high-frequency words; use of context; drawing on memory of what words look like; knowledge of word parts and structures such as prefixes, suffixes, root words, plurals, and verb endings)

- Is the student able to demonstrate this knowledge consistently?

Tony 3/9	Pauses at unknown word Begins by sounding out first letter, pauses again, looks through word to end Makes an attempt – but does not check correct meaning.	Susan 3/9	Immediately seeks help from teacher Needs prompting to use strategies of looking for known words and breaking in to syllables Not independent or confident

Teacher–student interview

Interviews are like a formal discussion where the teacher inquires into a student's learning and knowledge of his or her learning by asking questions, such as:

1. What do you do when you come to a word you don't recognize? Why?
   - Can you figure out which part of the word you get stuck on?
   - Are there some particular sounds that you often find hard? What are they?
   - Are there some particular letter combinations that you find difficult to figure out? What are they?
2. How do you know what to do when you come to a word you don't recognize?
   - What do you think about when you get stuck on a word?
   - What strategies do you use to try to figure it out?
3. How do you know if you get the word right?
4. What do you do when you have tried but you still can't figure out a word? Why?

The teacher records the student's responses for later analysis, aiming to find out:

- Did the student have word-recognition strategies to draw on?
- Did the student know why some of these strategies work better than others?
- Did the student understand that good readers often use more than one strategy to figure out an unfamiliar word?

- Was the student relying on teacher prompts or was he or she able to do this independently?
- Was the student able to identify areas where he or she would like teacher support?

The teacher can then discuss the results with the student and together decide on suitable learning goals (see page 22).

Explain what you did when you came to this word and you didn't recognize it.

You've stopped here, can you tell me why? What are you going to now?

What were you thinking when you first got stuck on this word?

Student demonstration

Students can use the think-aloud method (described on page 25) to reveal their thinking to the teacher as they try to figure out an unknown word.

The teacher can record the student's explanation on tape, make brief notes, or use a checklist of predetermined criteria. This information can be used to help make decisions about what to teach. Teachers will also use the information to provide feedback to students about their use of word-recognition strategies and to assist them to set learning goals that will help develop those strategies.

Metacognitive comprehension instruction

Using the instructional strategies, practices, and approaches that are described in chapter 1 and chapter 6, teachers can plan to teach strategies that students can use to figure out new words. In particular, the use of modeling, collaborative use, and guided practice can be used to support independent practice. As they become more confident and aware of what they are doing, students take over the responsibility for using the strategies, demonstrating their knowledge by their ability to explain and model strategies to others and to engage in discussions about words – both inside and outside planned lessons.

Teachers can select target strategies for instruction, then:

- explain what the strategy is and how it can be used to figure out what a word says
- model what to do when the students come to a word they do not recognize, using the target strategy
- provide opportunities for students to practice the strategy in a variety of contexts, with the amount of guidance or support depending on individual or group needs
- encourage students to model word-recognition strategies for other students. As they do so, students should be encouraged to explain what they are doing and why.

Integrated instruction that will develop student cognitive and metacognitive knowledge about word recognition teaches students:

- what strategies they are learning
- when and how to apply the strategies
- why using these strategies is worthwhile.

Whenever possible, the activities used for teaching word-recognition strategies need to be in the context of real reading. This allows students to meet new challenges and try out problem solving around unrecognized words while also providing for practice and review of knowledge.

Teaching key strategies for word recognition

Over time, teachers will explain and model a variety of strategies. Students should be encouraged to come to lessons equipped with a notebook or a whiteboard to record and explore any words that they were not able to recognize instantly. Teachers and students together can chart the strategies that assist them with word recognition.

When we come to a word we don't recognize, we can try one or more of the following strategies:
Look at the sounds and letters at the beginning of the word.
Look at the sounds and letters in the middle and end of the word.
Break the word into syllables and sound out each syllable.
Look for common letter combinations within the word.
Look for a word family in the word then check to see if you know a word that rhymes and that would make sense.
Look for a word family in the word, then think of a word you know with a similar spelling pattern.
Look at the structure of the word. Do you see a root or base word? A prefix? A suffix? An ending?
Break the word into syllables. Sound out each syllable and blend the syllable parts to work out the word.

Charts like this are most effective when they are developed *with* the students as a result of teacher explanation, modeling, discussion, and scaffolded practice. If students are presented with a chart of predetermined strategies, these will not be as meaningful (and not as well used) as a chart that students have helped to develop.

As students draw on these word-recognition strategies, they will need many opportunities to practice individual strategies. However, teachers need to remind students that strategies are rarely used on their own. Depending on the level of challenge, several strategies are often used at once.

Teachers need to use caution when considering how much instruction to provide and in what form: too much instructional focus on the components of words may detract from the focus on deriving meaning (see the following chapters). Also, the further the instruction is removed from reading real texts, the more difficulty students may have with integrating their learning into their reading.

Independent, partner, and group activities

The following activities can be conducted orally or in written form independently or in groups of various sizes. They are intended to lead to fast and effortless word recognition, giving students more time to attend to meaning.

The activities can be used with words that students have not recognized during the normal reading program, including their independent reading. Encourage them to keep an individual record of words they did not recognize or had difficulty recognizing, especially in their subject-specific reading. This provides a record of the types of words they find difficult to recognize and becomes the word source for activities, games, reading, and writing.

Alternatively, students can be encouraged to keep logs for self-monitoring (see "Individual student reflective records" below) in which they also record those strategies that assisted word recognition. Provide opportunities for discussion within activities that allow the students to think aloud as they explain what they are doing and why.

In all of these activities, it is important to scaffold student performance to provide just the right amount of support as students attempt to practice the skills that they have been taught. When learning is being scaffolded, it is important not to let students struggle unassisted for long. Instead, provide just enough support to nudge them on (for example, by using a question, a prompt, or a visual aid) without actually doing the work for them. Take every opportunity to let students learn to take charge of their own learning.

The activities described below are provided as models that you can adapt and share with the students before they start an activity. Writing the learning goals on a chart or on the board helps the students to keep them in mind as they work.

By explaining, students develop a metacognitive understanding of word-recognition strategies rather than skills that may not be robust enough on their own to help them figure out words in a variety of situations.

Create opportunities for students to explain *what* they are learning, *why* it is important, and *how* they have used their learning as they encounter words they don't recognize. These opportunities can be found before, during, and after the activities are used.

You can also encourage students to take a learning goal and develop possible success criteria for that goal. For example, they can use the stem "We will know we've achieved this when we can …" to prompt their thinking about what they are trying to achieve. See page 22 for more information about learning goals and success criteria.

Individual student reflective records

We are learning to:
  • develop an awareness of our own learning.

Students can keep individual logs in which they record difficult words, state why a word was difficult, and explain how they solved it. This can be done in a notebook or on a bookmark that is later discussed with you, another student, or with a group.

Word Recognition Log		
• words I didn't recognize	• parts I found hard	• strategies to assist me

Developing charts from group instruction

We are learning to:

- develop an awareness of our own learning
- identify the strategies we use to figure out words.

We didn't recognize these words ...	We used these strategies to help us
mound	It looks like sound but starts with m. (analogy)
unique	It ends like my friend's name Monique. (analogy). The letter u can be long or short, so I'll try both to see which one sounds right.
development	We found the root word (develop) and the suffix (-ment), then blended them together.

You can add to this chart during reading and as a result of metacognitive comprehension instruction. Refer to it later as you and the students discuss these questions:

- What is the word?
- What parts made it difficult to recognize?
- What strategies assisted word recognition?

You can also make the words into flash cards, cut-up letters, word family games, words that rhyme, a word wall, individual spelling lists, vocabulary study, partner quizzes from word walls, and word sorts (sorting words with similar sounds or according to categories – initial sounds, vowel sounds, number of syllables, common spelling patterns, final sounds, medial sounds).

Exploring syllables

We are learning to:

- use strategies to decode multi-syllabic words
- identify the vowels that help divide the syllables in multi-syllabic words
- use syllabification strategies to help us pronounce new words.

As students read increasingly complex informational texts, they encounter many new multi-syllabic words. For some students, decoding skills break down when they are confronted with multi-syllabic words because they cannot figure out the syllables. Use mini-lessons to explain syllables and to demonstrate that, for example, each syllable has one vowel sound, and that finding the vowels can help to break a word into syllables. Explain that some syllables may have one vowel (*cot, sub*) and others may have a group of vowels (*coat, head*) but still only one sound. It is often a good idea to teach syllabification strategies using known words first and then show students how they can apply this knowledge to unknown words.

Use mini-lessons to teach some useful guides for syllabification. They could be based on dictionary pronunciation guides that show accent or stress, for example:

- The accent shows the syllable that is stressed (heard most clearly *con*/*ference*).
- In words with a prefix or suffix, the accent falls on the root word (*un*/*kind*).
- In compound words, the accent falls on or within the first word (*foot*/*ball*).
- When only one consonant occurs between the vowels, divide the word before the consonant (*a*/*void*).
- When two or more consonants appear in the middle of the word, the syllables divide between these consonants (*cor*/*rect*).

Word changing

We are learning to:

- recognize that words and their sounds can change by altering one or more of the letters
- attend to the sounds that various letters (or letter combinations) make.

Give the students a word and set a "rule" for making changes, for example, changing the first letter only. Ask students to say the original word and listen to how the new word sounds: *clap, flap, slap; ship, chip; cast, vast, past, last.*

Move on to changing other letters, staying with one letter at a time: *claws, flaws, flows, floss, gloss, gross, grass, glass, class, clasp, clamp …*

This activity can also be repeated with middle letters, ending letters, and by altering two letters that make one sound such as a digraph or vowel combination. In these instances, focus students on the sounds that were altered, as well as the replacement sound. Encourage them to compile their own list for this activity – words can come from their own reading and be shared with a partner.

Exploring pseudo words

We are learning to:

- use what we know about letters and the sounds they represent to sound out words
- read words we have never seen before.

Pseudo words are words that look like real words but are not real because they have no meaning. Examples can be simple or complex, such as *plam, wef, shumble, cragement.* By exploring pseudo words, students are forced to practice their decoding skills. They need to use analogies with known chunks (for example, *-umble, -ment*) and draw on their ability to associate letters with their sounds and blend the sounds to pronounce the word. This means that students are working with the sounding-out strategy, which is one that good readers do well. Pseudo words can either be provided by you or by the students themselves. As students attempt to use the sounding-out skills, they can verbalize and explain their thinking to others.

Investigating common combinations

We are learning to:

- instantly recognize common letter combinations
- instantly recognize the sounds made by common letter combinations.

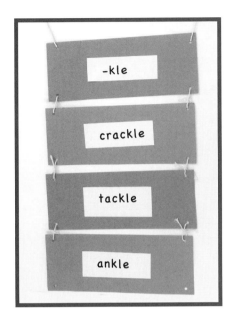

Provide instruction through modeling and explanation to ensure that students are able to recognize common English letter combinations such as those in:

- word families (*-op, -ake*)
- digraphs (*ch, sh, th*)
- blends (*s, l, r words*)
- word endings (*-s, -ed, -ing*)
- common letter patterns that go together (*-ble, -ible, -able*).

Automatic recognition of these combinations leads to more rapid decoding of new words that contain them. Encourage students to explore examples of combinations as they encounter written text. This could include developing group charts, mobiles, and other visual displays of words that have common combinations. Remember, the more opportunities that students have to practice rapid recognition of sounds and combinations, the more quickly and effortlessly they will be able to recognize new words.

This task can also be extended to include suffix, prefix, and base or root word activities using words with common combinations, for example: *tackle – tackled, tackling, mistackle; photograph, photocopy.*

Exploring word families

We are learning to:

- use known word families to figure out new words.

This means teaching students to call on their knowledge of onset and rime, word families, syllabification, and analogy to known words (onset and rime – an initial consonant followed by a vowel with subsequent consonants – *c/at, p/art*).

These activities explore the sounds made by different word parts, which can later be applied (used to make analogies) to recognize a wider variety of words. For example, if students know the rime *-eat* as in *heat*, they can use this knowledge to figure out *beat, meat, wheat, seat, repeat, beaten, wheaten, heated*. This activity can be used to explore content-area words, such as those found in science or mathematics.

Start by providing a mini-lesson on one or two rimes (or word families) that students have difficulty with. Tell the students about the rime and the sound it makes and provide examples of words with this rime. Following this, a variety of activities can be used to reinforce awareness and knowledge of word families, including:

- Word families can be charted and displayed for the students to refer to.
- A "word family" or rime dictionary that contains lists of words with a common family or rime can be complied. This can become a class, group, or individual record.
- The students can play card games where they take turns saying a word that contains a given rime.
- Rhyme games – "I am thinking of a group of words that rhyme with *ant.*" – students listen to the sound and then give 2, 3, or 4 words that rhyme. Alternatively, keep going around the group until no one can think of any other rhymes.
- Partner games – encourage students to complete games where they have to make connections between letters, adjacent letters, letter combinations, and rimes.

Discovering prefixes, suffixes, and root words

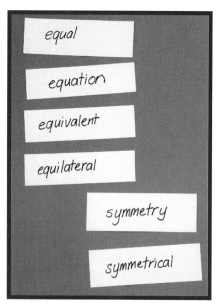

We are learning to:

- identify the sound sequences that make up prefixes, suffixes, and root words
- automatically recognize prefixes, suffixes, and root words
- use what we know about prefixes, suffixes, and root words to help recognize new words.

Prefixes, suffixes, and commonly occurring root words (and their meanings) can be taught as recurring combinations of letters that should be committed to memory. Students need to have many opportunities to find these recurring combinations in their reading. The more opportunities students have to explore prefixes, suffixes, and root words, the more likely they will recognize them as whole sounds and will not need to sound them out letter by letter.

For example, the word *dissatisfied* uses the prefix *dis-*, the root word *satisfy*, and the suffix *-ed*.

Students can build a chart to record these combinations. They can come from their reading and writing, cross-curricula studies, or from words selected by the teacher to support specifically targeted instruction.

Prefix	Root word	Suffix
dis-	agree	-ment
un-	fashion	-able
de-	construct	-ion

See also the discussion on pages 85 and 86 in chapter 3.
See appendix 3.1 (page 106) and 3.2 (page 107) for a list of common prefixes and suffixes, and their meanings.

When readers struggle

Word recognition is a critical component in learning to read and comprehend texts. There are many reasons why some students acquire word-recognition skills more quickly than others. These may include:

- the amount of exposure students have had to text (being read to as well as independent reading)
- the amount of deliberately planned instruction they have received in the early years (with particular focus on letter–sound relationships, onset and rime, rhymes, jingles)
- the ability to self-monitor their reading
- their development of a repertoire of strategies and an awareness of how to use them
- the amount of exposure students have had to rich and varied vocabulary
- the students' proficiency in using visual and graphophonic sources of information
- the need to learn English if this is not the home language.

Teachers need to be aware of when and how "breakdowns" occur in order to provide the most effective instruction. Students too need to know about the aspects of word recognition that are causing them to struggle so they can be metacognitive in their learning.

For students who struggle, teachers will need to draw on a variety of assessment tools to find out more about their letter–sound and word-recognition needs. Examples of these assessments include assessments of letter–sound, sound–letter knowledge, initial, medial, and end blends and pseudo words (Allcock, 2004; Clay, 1991, 1998; Cunningham, 2004).

Generally, these tools would not be used to assess older students, but when used in conjunction with other broader assessments, they may provide useful information for teachers as they plan instruction for students who are really struggling with letters, sounds, and word recognition.

Dictation is another way of assessing student knowledge of letter–sound relationships. When sentences are read aloud to students and students write the sentences down, teachers can see which letter–sound relationships and combinations students are having difficulty with. A check against words containing these sounds will enable teachers to decide on the most appropriate way to build this knowledge into the lessons.

Teachers may also wish to develop their own assessments using structured observations or interview questions based on the following areas, each of which is useful when a reader encounters unknown words:

- onset and rime or word families
- syllabification
- prefixes and suffixes
- root/base words.

Students struggling with word recognition benefit from teaching that focuses on word-reading processes aimed to increase their knowledge, skills, and awareness of ways to recognize words previously encountered but not retained, along with new words that they may not have encountered before. Students who struggle need opportunities to find the fun and learning that comes from playing with words. They need to be included in these activities too.

In addition to regular reading comprehension instruction, students who are struggling with word recognition will benefit from a dedicated time within the daily literacy time that focuses specifically on their needs. A daily ten-minute slot will be an important part of organizing instruction to be responsive to students' needs.

The following section provides some suggestions for metacognitive instruction for figuring out words. This is not intended to be an exhaustive list and should be viewed in conjunction with the examples in the first part of this chapter and in the suggestions for able readers. Teachers will need to monitor the effectiveness of the lessons and modify them accordingly. As with the activities above, sharing the learning goals and creating opportunities for students to explain what they are learning as they work will reinforce their learning and they will develop a deeper, metacognitive awareness of their learning processes.

Identifying letter–sound relationships

While there are twenty-six letters in the English alphabet, research indicates that there are between forty-three and forty-six different sounds, depending on the pronunciation used in different regions and countries. What this means is that students need to be aware that there may be more than one sound for any letter. This is important for older students who may not have developed a firm foundation in phonics, especially in the area of sound–symbol relationships, in the early grades. Providing instruction that helps students to "think through" the options to read words will help them to overcome some of the difficulties they experience with decoding (and spelling) new words. This is especially true with vowel sounds in English, which often have more than one sound for a given letter. It should be noted, however, that in Spanish, vowel sounds have a single and relatively invariable sound. This may result in Spanish-speaking students having difficulty with various vowel sounds, substituting them with Spanish vowel sounds as they transfer from Spanish to English.

Using a problem-solving approach, explore the sounds associated with given letters, drawing the students' attention to possible sound–letter relationships and words where they occur. In the following example, grade 4 students study the various sounds the letter *a* can make.

Prompt the students to notice that *a* can make different sounds. If students notice other regional (or family) differences, discuss these and add them to the chart, using a new column if necessary. Some Canadian speakers, for example, pronounce *aunt* in more than one way depending on their heritage or region. Closer exploration will show that sometimes *a* can have two different sounds within one word (*against, Aidan, animal*).

At this stage, you may wish to highlight some of the phonics rules, for example, the use of the "magic" *e* (vowel–consonant–silent *e* pattern). When an *e* is added to a word or syllable with a vowel and a consonant, the vowel sound changes from a short to a long sound. Examples include *hat* and *hate*, and *pal* and *pale*. It is important to remind students that while phonics rules can be learned and are useful, they are not always reliable and absolute.

Opportunities for teachers and students to explore the vowel sound similarities and differences, to talk about the differences, and to find and demonstrate other examples are important aspects of a teaching program that builds student awareness and knowledge of letter–sound relationships.

As you work with the students to find and discuss examples of sound–letter combinations, they can be recorded on a group chart, a word wall, a page of an individual students learning log or reading journal, or as a presentation prepared by group members to be shared with the class.

"a"

| a — a word to use in a sentence — A meteor, We read about a mining community |
| a — a syllable used to begin another word — again, around, arise |
| a — makes the sound of its name — cake, make, take, shake, shaken, taken |
| There is an e that helps me with these ones. |

We are learning to identify the letters that make or change the sound of *a*

a-e	— the vowel-consonant-silent e rule — there is one other letter (a consonant) between the vowel and the e and it makes the long a sound
-ay	— at the end of a word — makes the long a sound — today, play
ai	— in the middle of a word or syllable — makes the long a sound — pain, painful
ar	— The letter r following a changes the sound of an a to an r sound — car, far, partner, cardinal number, flowchart

We have learned

The vowel+consonant+e rule
An r following an a changes the a to an r sound
There are lots of different sounds made by the letter a!

Group members' signatures: ___Aiden   Tim   Jenny___

In conclusion, the pronunciation of vowel sounds will vary depending on local pronunciation and language conventions. The important learning takes place when students are involved in recognizing and talking about these variations and when they display examples and exceptions for future reading and spelling reference. An exploratory approach to phonics and spelling will help them to recognize the sounds and to be aware of the ways that letters and sounds are related. It will also help students to understand that letter sounds are not finite and absolute.

Focusing on short and long vowel sounds

Teaching that deliberately draws attention to the ways of writing short and long vowel sounds is essential as students learn to use their knowledge of sound–letter relationships to recognize unknown words. There are many different ways that long vowel sounds can be written, and students need many opportunities to learn about and practice them. Some examples include:

Find words with the long a sound:

beak	feather
kilogram	weigh
range	above
mountain	water
each	they
advance	prey
average	opaque

- Students are given a list of words and asked to identify those words containing long vowel sounds. (Lists can be compiled by the teacher or by other students within the group.) The students highlight the letters that make the long vowel sound. Select words that appear in the students' current reading and that illustrate a sound they are studying.
- Read aloud words containing a specific vowel sound. Students spell each word and underline the letters that make up the focus vowel sound.
- Vowel sounds are listed on cards and students use these to write more words that follow each sound.
- Students sort words with the same vowel sounds from a list that is either written down or read orally.

Blending consonants

Where students have difficulty in hearing or pronouncing the sounds in consonant blends, teaching will need to include explicit instruction on how two or three consonants form a blend. Teaching will demonstrate that blends are two sounds that are written with two different letters.

They may occur at the beginning, middle, or end of words. These are called initial, medial, and final blends. Provide many opportunities for students to speak, hear, and look for blends, choosing two or three a week to focus on and taking every opportunity to practice recognizing and pronouncing them during reading and writing instruction.

Students can work in groups, with a partner, or individually to compile a record of consonant blends. They can group words according to common blends; create lists of words that have common blends at the beginning, middle, and end of a word; and can practice reading and pronouncing these to one another.

Double-letter blends	Triple-letter blends
spell	street
spot	stretch
sponge	strain
speak	strip
sphere	structure

Clusters of letters

There are a number of letter clusters that students can memorize to make connections to new or unknown words. Teaching needs to include learning to recognize, pronounce, and blend familiar clusters of letters, common affixes (prefixes and suffixes), syllables, and spelling patterns. With the students, build up displays to exemplify common clusters, and engage in games, quizzes, and "competitions" to find and pronounce new words with common clusters.

Letter clusters:

-ake	-ight
make	frightful
shaken	highlight
mistake	unsightly
	plight
-ance	
appearance	-ange
nuisance	strange
performance	rearrange
importance	

Syllables

Some students do not know how to break unfamiliar and longer words into syllables and how to pronounce syllables. While this strategy is often associated with learning to write words, it is also extremely important in learning to read and recognize words. Students needing support will benefit from practice in segmenting words into parts or syllables then blending and pronouncing them. Teaching can also show how they can draw on their knowledge of letter sounds, blends, and clusters of letters.

It is important that instruction aims to encourage students to use a wide variety of word-recognition strategies as they read. Some of these strategies have been described earlier in the chapter but are repeated here because they are particularly effective for students who struggle with decoding and word recognition.

Use of analogy

Encouraging students to explain their thinking out loud provides you with an insight into their understanding, while at the same time helping them to clarify the processes that they are using. Examples include:

- recognizing how spellings of unknown words are similar to words they already know – "I know the spelling of *bake*. If I replaced *b* with *sh* the word would be *shake*. Therefore, the word I am struggling with will be *shaken*."

- using sight words to read new words by analogy – "I know *cat* so this word will be *flat*."

Development of sight words

Skilled readers focus on words, not individual letters, because they recognize many words at a glance. You can provide opportunities for students to develop their sight word memory by focusing on both recognizing words and pronouncing them. This helps the students to make and retain connections between the written form of a word (what it looks like), its pronunciation (what it sounds like), its spelling, and its meaning. As students increase the number of words they recognize on sight, they begin to read without having to decode and can give more attention to comprehension. There are many published lists of common sight words and activities that will help students to memorize words, but with older students, it is important to ensure that the activities are appropriate to their age, relevant to their interests, and where possible, connected with the reading required in class.

Use of context clues

You can teach students to use context clues to help predict an unknown word. Prediction may be based on clues provided from a preceding sentence, other words in the sentence, and illustrations. Remind students to use their prior knowledge to help them predict a word from the context.

This approach has limitations. If students do not have the word in their spoken vocabulary they are unlikely to be able to guess it. In addition, not all texts provide adequate clues or clues that the student can recognize and relate to. Students may predict a word that will make sense, but it may not be the word that the author used: they must use context in tandem with their word-recognition strategies. For these reasons, this strategy is most effective when used in conjunction with others, such as using initial letters and analogies.

Increasing the quality and quantity of reading

Students who struggle with word recognition benefit from as much practice in reading as can be fitted into the day. One effect of reading more and more is that students will increase the speed of their reading. This is particularly important in preventing reading difficulties where decoding is slow, deliberate, and not fluent. Readers who struggle to recognize words often lose interest and give up easily, thus falling even further behind in their learning. Text difficulty (see below) is a critical factor in selecting texts for students who are struggling.

While repeated reading of texts that students already know is beneficial (and links to fluency, see chapter 4), students who need practice at decoding unknown words benefit from reading a wide variety of new and interesting texts, including texts that they have not encountered before. For new (unseen) text reading to be beneficial, the text needs to be at a reading level where students are making no more than six errors in every hundred words. Ask the students to read a passage of one hundred or more words and count the errors to ensure that the text is at the appropriate level. Students can be trained to use this method themselves to judge the difficulty of a text. If they come across six or more words that they can't figure out quickly, the text is too hard. Many students will already be familiar with this method, but may need discrete prompting to continue using it.

Extending able readers

Even students who have well-developed strategies for recognizing unknown words will encounter new and challenging words as they read more widely. Take opportunities to assist these students to develop their strategies further. A primary aim will be to foster a lively interest in and curiosity about words: where they come from, how they can be built up from parts, how they sound when spoken aloud, how they look, and how writers can play with their structure to create humor. The following examples show how this can be fostered.

Finding challenging words

Encourage students to keep a record of words they find challenging. These should be words that they either did not know or that have interesting, difficult, or unusual spelling patterns, combinations of letters, or multiple meanings. Encourage the students to highlight the parts of the words that made them challenging and ask them to share these with other members of their reading group.

Students will need time to discuss the words presented by their peers, to suggest strategies for word recognition, and to recognize similarities and differences between these and other words that the students know.

Discussion such as this will lead to increased awareness of words and how words work and will heighten the students' understanding of strategies and approaches that assist word recognition.

Exploring spelling patterns

Provide learning opportunities to explore specific spelling patterns in many common words, and consequently, the role of these patterns in learning to recognize words. For example, this could include a focus on the many different ways the *r* controlled *er* sound can be written (*er, ir, or, ur, ure*). Students can look for patterns and examples among these sounds as a way of connecting word-recognition skills to their spelling program.

Some writers make a feature of playing with spelling patterns for effect. Roald Dahl does this in *The BFG*, a novel that many students may have read. Encourage them to explore the spelling patterns and substitutions that Dahl exploited to create "new" words. For example, a *snozzcumber* is a vegetable that tastes *disgusterous and foulsome*.

Talk about the knowledge and strategies students use as they figure out new words.

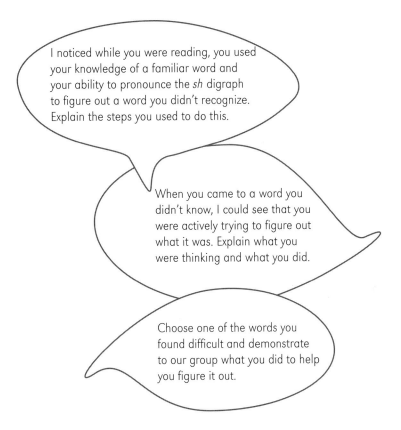

I noticed while you were reading, you used your knowledge of a familiar word and your ability to pronounce the *sh* digraph to figure out a word you didn't recognize. Explain the steps you used to do this.

When you came to a word you didn't know, I could see that you were actively trying to figure out what it was. Explain what you were thinking and what you did.

Choose one of the words you found difficult and demonstrate to our group what you did to help you figure it out.

Other suggestions

There are many ways that students can be encouraged to explore and play with words and how they are constructed. Students themselves may already use board and electronic games that require knowledge of word structure. Those who use text messaging will be very adept at using contractions to spell a message in as few letters as possible. Ask the students to construct games and challenges for one another that use and build on their knowledge, for example, a game that involves figuring out regular and innovative contractions. The word-changing activity on page 51 and the pseudo-word activity on page 52 can be extended by students themselves, for example, by making new rules for word changing and by inventing pronounceable psuedo words for one another to read.

Developing metacognitive awareness

All of the activities described above encourage students to develop a metacognitive awareness of the strategies that they can use to figure out unknown words. By making instruction metacognitive, teachers can take advantage of the many opportunities to develop students' awareness of what they are learning. This mostly happens through high-quality dialogue between teacher and students and among students themselves.

Teachers can plan for dialogue that focuses on developing students' understanding of word-recognition strategies (what to do) and on encouraging an active and informed problem-solving approach (how to do it) to figuring out unknown words. When students know what they are doing as they read and why it is important, they gain control of their own learning.

Summary

This chapter has focused on one aspect of metacognitive comprehension instruction, namely providing instruction that is deliberately planned to assist students to learn to recognize words. Learning to recognize words is central to reading: unless the reader can recognize individual words, he or she can not process them into the sentences and paragraphs that make up texts. If students can read words quickly and automatically, then word recognition will not interfere with comprehension. Effective instruction involves equipping students with knowledge, strategies, and skills that they can apply when they encounter unfamiliar words at the same time as giving them many, many opportunities to read extended texts in which they can practice using what they have learned.

References and recommended reading

Allcock, J. (2004). *Switch on to Spelling*. Paremata, New Zealand: M.J.A. Publishing.

Baumann, J. F., Edwards, E. C., Font, G., Tereshinski, C. A., Kame'enui, E. J., and Olejnik, S. (2002). "Teaching Morphemic and Contextual Analysis to Fifth-grade Students". *Reading Research Quarterly*, 37(2), pp. 150–176.

Clay, M. M. (1991). *Becoming Literate: The Construction of Inner Control*. Portsmouth, New Hampshire: Heinemann.

Clay, M. M. (1998). *By Different Paths to Common Outcomes*. York, Maine: Stenhouse.

Cunningham, P. M. (2004). *Phonics They Use: Words for Reading and Writing*, (4th ed.). Boston: Pearson/Allyn & Bacon.

Dahl, K. L., Scharer, P. L., Lawson, L. L., and Grogan, P. R. (2001). *Rethinking Phonics: Making the Best Teaching Decisions.* Portsmouth, New Hampshire: Heinemann.

Ehri, L. (1995). "Phases of Development in Learning to Read Words by Sight". *Journal of Research in Reading*, 18(2), pp. 116–125.

Mesmer, H. A. E. and Griffith, P. L. (2005). "Everybody's Selling It – But What Is Explicit, Systematic Phonics Instruction?" *The Reading Teacher*, 59(4), pp. 366–376.

National Institute of Child Health and Human Development (NICHD). (2000). *Report of the National Reading Panel. Teaching Children to Read: Reports of the Subgroups* (NIH Publication No. 00-4769). Washington, DC: U.S. Government Printing Office.

National Reading Panel (2000). *Report of the National Reading Panel*. Washington, DC: U.S. Government Printing Office. www.nationalreadingpanel.org

Nicholson, T. (2005). *At the Cutting Edge: The Importance of Phonemic Awareness in Learning to Read and Spell.* (2nd ed.) Wellington, New Zealand: NZCER Press.

Pressley, M. (2006). *Reading Instruction That Works: The Case for Balanced Teaching.* (3rd ed.) New York, New York: The Guilford Press.

Rasinski, T. V. et al. (2000). *Teaching Word Recognition, Spelling, and Vocabulary: Strategies from The Reading Teacher*. Newark, Delaware: International Reading Association.

3

Working with Vocabulary Strategies

Readers cannot comprehend what they are reading without knowing what most of the words mean. This chapter explores how teaching of strategies for learning vocabulary can be integrated into classroom reading instruction and cross-curricula instruction in grades 3 to 8. While vocabulary instruction is important for all students, some students will require more or varied instruction according to their particular needs.

Key messages for teachers

- Vocabulary knowledge is a critical aspect of reading comprehension because words carry most of the meaning in a text.

- Students' prior knowledge plays an important role in vocabulary acquisition and use, as does the context in which the words are used and the number of encounters a student has had with a word.

- Many new words are learned indirectly. However, some new or barely familiar words and their meanings need to be taught directly.

- Students need to learn strategies that will assist them as they encounter unfamiliar vocabulary when they read, both during reading instruction and in content areas (for example, science, social studies, health). These strategies will give them access to the meaning of the words they read independently.

- All teachers have a responsibility for developing their students' vocabulary, particularly students with limited experience or those for whom English is not the first language.

- Systematic approaches to vocabulary instruction do make a difference. It is possible to narrow achievement gaps in vocabulary knowledge and this in turn enhances reading comprehension.

- When students are actively involved in their own learning, they are more likely to develop metacognitive understandings about the meanings of words.

Teaching vocabulary

Knowing the learning needs of students is paramount to all instruction, including vocabulary instruction. Alongside this, teachers need to know what words to teach and how to teach them: they need to understand (and be able to teach students) the use of metacognitive word-learning strategies.

Instruction is most effective when it provides multiple exposures to the words being taught. Students need many opportunities to interact with new vocabulary so that the words become part of their schema and they have the confidence and knowledge to retain, recognize, understand, and use these words appropriately.

There are many opportunities to teach vocabulary throughout the day. While some opportunities are ad hoc and incidental, many are intentional and planned.

Much research (Baumann and Kame'enui, 2004; Elley, 1997; Graves and Watts-Taffe, 2002; McKeown and Beck, 2004; Nagy, 2005; National Reading Panel, 2000; RAND, 2002) indicates that leaving vocabulary development only to incidental learning can be problematic and does not lead to improved student achievement. This is largely because incidental learning relies too heavily on student prior knowledge. Therefore, it is important to provide vocabulary instruction that is planned, explicit, and deliberate. Such instruction should also impart a sense of excitement about words within a language-rich environment.

Planned instruction also aims to provides a breadth of information to students. This is particularly important with words that have nuances of meaning or application that may not be apparent until students have been exposed to multiple meanings in many different contexts, including figurative and idiomatic uses. Vocabulary needs to be presented in a range of contexts, engaging students actively in learning about words.

Other researchers (Anderson, 1996; Stahl, 1998) believe that increasing the amount of reading that students do is one of the most influential ways of increasing their vocabulary. Teaching programs that offer regular independent reading opportunities, along with teachers reading aloud to students, provide excellent settings for learning vocabulary. In this sense, the incidental learning that occurs through wide reading is significant: it is not possible to "teach" all the words and their nuances that students need to know. Researchers suggest that the best way to increase exposure to vocabulary is to increase the quantity of reading that students do (and hear) across a wide variety of text types.

Teachers own use of language and their ability to model and use complex language is another important factor in exposing students to new and challenging vocabulary.

Identifying student needs

As discussed in chapter 1, teachers collect data about the strengths and needs of their students before they decide what to teach. They can do this by using a variety of vocabulary assessment tools (a number of which are available commercially) and through ongoing formative assessment (observation, questioning, discussion, marking work, collaboratively setting learning goals and success criteria, giving feedback). The data will help them to determine the best way of teaching the knowledge and skills that their students need. Teaching includes both direct instruction and the follow-up support students receive through independent and group activities. This means that instruction (teacher and student directed) occurs both within and outside planned lessons.

Ongoing observations

These are observations that can be carried out in the course of the school day and across different subject areas. Teachers can use checklists or anecdotal records to answer questions, such as the following:

- What behavior does the student demonstrate when faced with vocabulary challenges?
- What words are causing difficulty for the student?
- What kinds of words seem to offer particular challenges? (for example, subject-specific words, multisyllabic words, words with Greek or Latin derivations)
- What words are being used incorrectly in the student's writing? Is this because the student is not fully aware of the meaning or usage of the word?

- What words cause problems when they are used in unfamiliar ways?
- What does the student's oral language reveal about his or her vocabulary?

The vocabulary a teacher identifies as causing difficulty for students is the vocabulary that needs to be taught.

Self-reporting of challenging vocabulary

New Words:

friction

Mach

inertia

momentum

aerodynamic

Valuable data can be gathered by teaching students to self-report vocabulary they have trouble with. When students have been asked to read an unseen text, they can use a bookmark, sticky note, or notebook to keep a record of the vocabulary that they found challenging. The students then meet with their reading group or the teacher to discuss the new vocabulary. The teacher and students then discuss this vocabulary during a group reading lesson to check the students' understandings of the words.

Targeted observations

Observations of this kind are planned and focused: the teacher observes while a student (alone or within a group) explains the strategies they used to figure out a word from an unseen text. Teachers can select one or two focus areas, then observe and record behaviors, such as the following:

- Is the student confident in explaining how to figure out the meaning of a word?
- Does the student enter into conversations about words or ask for help to understand a word without prompting by the teacher?
- Does the student's explanation show a good knowledge of word structure? For example, is the student able to identify and use prefixes, suffixes, root words, verb tenses, and plural forms to help figure out meaning?
- Does the student's explanation demonstrate the use of semantic knowledge to assist with vocabulary? For example, is the student able to:
  - consider the word in relation to the words and sentences around it?
  - look for clues such as synonyms or antonyms in the surrounding text?

- consider the word in relation to the overall content of the text?
- read on to see if the meaning of unknown vocabulary is revealed?
- read back (reread) to look for clues to help figure out unknown vocabulary?
- Does the student's explanation demonstrate the use of syntactic knowledge to assist with vocabulary? For example, is the student able to:
  - predict the meaning of the word based on its grammatical function?
  - read on or reread to check syntactic accuracy while at the same time searching for overall meaning?
- Are there other strategies suggested by the student? If so, what are they?

The data will help the teacher to identify words to teach as well as reveal key vocabulary strategies that students would benefit from. It will also reveal the extent to which students are able to apply metacognitive strategies as they approach challenging vocabulary.

The teacher can then discuss the data with students and together decide on suitable learning goals (see page 22).

Teacher: (pointing at *plight*) I noticed you paused before you read this word. What were you thinking when you did that?

Student: At first I just thought I didn't know it. Then I looked at it again and realized that I knew how to pronounce it – I recognized the *-ight* sound and with *pl* in front, so I could say *plight*.

Teacher: That's a very useful strategy, using what you know about parts of the word. Were you able to figure out what it meant?

Student: No, I guessed it could mean *number*, but I wasn't sure.

Teacher: That's a reasonable guess. I'll show you how I look for clues in the text. I reread that part, and the words that helped me were *sold* and *slavery*, as well as the description of working more than twelve hours a day in a factory. These clues made me think that the conditions were really bad. I put bad conditions into the sentence, and it made sense. I figured that this is what *plight* would mean. I checked by reading on, and this made sense – he was speaking out about the bad conditions and fighting against child labour.

Student: Yeah, that makes sense to me now.

Teacher: Let's make this a new learning goal for you: figuring out the meanings of words by using clues in the text.

from "Making a Difference" by Rebecca Green, Power Zone* *Leaving Your Mark*

Metacognitive comprehension instruction
What words should I teach?

In addition to drawing on data gathered directly from students, it is helpful to draw on the work of researchers who have identified words that students need to know – words that need to be taught if they are not already in students' reading vocabularies. Beck, McKeown, and Kucan (2002) described three tiers of words in a mature, literate individual's vocabulary. These are not word lists, more a guide for identifying and thinking about which words to teach.

Tier 1 words

These are basic words that many students will know even before they start school, and they seldom need a great deal of instruction. They are words that are used frequently, so students encounter them regularly. Examples include words such as *mother, brother, car, sky, walk, adventure*. Students who are learning English may require specific instruction with these words.

Tier 2 words

These words are of high frequency for mature language users. They are words that appear frequently in texts and for which students must have some conceptual understanding. They are encountered in many contexts and are important for students to know and be able to use. They can be explained in terms that the students know. Generally speaking, if the words used to define the new word are likely to be unknown then that word is too hard. Tier 2 words should be taught to students. Examples include *reluctant, complex, estimate, characteristic,* and many thousands more.

Tier 3 words

These words are subject-specific. They are often found in technical texts. Examples include *rhizome, schist, efflorescence, macron*. They are not widely encountered or needed for most general reading. Therefore, instruction of these words should be on an "as needed" basis (for example, when approaching a new concept in science or a topic in geography). It would not be useful or efficient to teach such words without the relevant context.

The critical point is that teachers should be deliberate about the selection of vocabulary for instruction.

Based on this research, teachers can focus on teaching tier 2 words for the majority of students. When selecting tier 2 words, teachers can preview the texts that they know their students will be reading. As they do so, they look for words that are important for comprehension. These include general words that the student needs to comprehend, cross-curricula vocabulary, words a student may know but might not fully understand, and words that show effective language use. The purpose is to equip the students with vocabulary that they will need to use – the vocabulary can't be used if it isn't known.

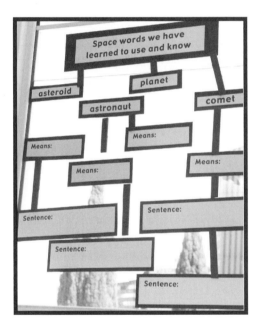

Academic vocabulary

There are many words used in teaching that allow teachers and students to talk and think in an academic manner. This "academic" vocabulary includes words such as *define, contrast, compare, divide, method*, and it requires instructional attention. It is especially important that students who are learning English are exposed to explicit instruction in these words. Using the tier analogy, many academic words would be considered tier 2 and tier 3, depending on the degree to which they will be used by the students.

Deciding which words to teach comes back to knowing the needs of students and their prior knowledge. Teachers' own knowledge of vocabulary and how it can be learned (for example, by working with root words) will help them to select the key tier 2 words that their students need to know. These words can be identified as teachers prepare lessons (including topic studies in subject areas) and as they select the texts they will use. The words can then be taught in lessons and reinforced in follow-up activities.

The low-frequency, specialized vocabulary in tier 3 can often be taught by simply telling the students the meaning of words that they are not likely to use themselves. In some contexts, specific instruction will be required to ensure students understand the concepts that are conveyed by specialized vocabulary. For example, in a mathematics or science lesson, teachers may wish to focus on teaching a small list of key words. In general, however, if a word is unlikely to be used reasonably often, teaching time is better spent on tier 2 words.

How vocabulary is learned

Learning new vocabulary does not happen from just one encounter with a new word. Researchers (Nagy and Scott, 2000) have concluded that many encounters in a variety of contexts are required before a person "knows" a word. In addition, these encounters should take place over an extended period so that students build up their confidence and ability with new vocabulary.

Beck, McKeown, and Kucan (2002) describe a protocol for teaching vocabulary that starts with the teacher providing a clear explanation of the meaning of a new word, then builds deeper understanding of how the word is used through modeling and scaffolded (teacher assisted) practice. Teachers encourage the students to think about and use new words meaningfully and appropriately through a variety of instructional practices.

Opportunities for vocabulary instruction

The focus of this section is on the deliberate teaching of vocabulary to aid comprehension. Within the reading comprehension lesson, there are four main opportunities for vocabulary instruction. These are:

1. **Vocabulary instruction in preparation for reading (a pre-reading activity)**

   This instruction prepares students for any challenging or new vocabulary that they will encounter. It often involves students previewing the text in anticipation of vocabulary challenges.

2. **Vocabulary instruction integrated within the reading comprehension lesson**

   This instruction occurs in the course of the reading comprehension lesson. Teachers and students identify challenges in vocabulary as the text is read. This is supported by discussion along with teacher and student modeling and practice of specific strategies to identify the meaning of the word.

3. Vocabulary instruction in response to reading

This instruction takes place after the reading lesson is completed. It requires students to work with new vocabulary encountered in the reading. The words students explore in this instruction are selected as a direct result of the challenges discovered throughout the lesson.

4. The mini-lesson

This instruction takes place where opportunities arise for specific lessons on vocabulary. Sometimes this is around a specific word type (for example, words that indicate the passage of time or the sequence of events), a specific strategy for deriving meaning (for example, knowledge of the prefix *dis*), a particular context (for example, words with multiple meanings) in which words are located, or a specific skill that students are struggling with. It can take place during the reading lesson or as a short stand-alone lesson.

Within each of these opportunities, the teacher provides a leading role, gradually releasing responsibility for this to the students.

Using instructional strategies and approaches

Teachers can use the instructional strategies, practices, and approaches described in chapter 1 and chapter 6 to teach strategies that students can use to acquire new vocabulary. In particular, modeling, collaborative use, and guided practice all support independent practice.

Modeling and thinking aloud

Modeling can be supported by use of the think-aloud strategy to allow teachers and students to share their processing. It is also an excellent way to show students how to ask effective questions to explore vocabulary.

Example: to show how the structural analysis of a word can lead to its meaning

- I know that the prefix *un* means not, so *unexplored* must mean not explored and *unsure* must mean not sure. (Modeling and thinking aloud)
- "Her expression was frosty" – I can see the word *frost* in here. Frost is cold. I think this could mean that her expression is cold. From my experience, a cold expression is not pleasant. (Modeling and thinking aloud)
- Can we find the root word? Is there a suffix? Prefix? Are there some clues in the word that we can use to help us? Is this a compound word? (Thinking aloud; collaborative use of a strategy)

Example: to explore the use of context clues

- Let's look at the information in the text. Can we infer the meaning of the word? What information assisted us? Were we able to draw on the sentence the word was in, the surrounding sentences, or were there definitions, examples, or synonyms within the text? (Thinking aloud; collaborative use of a strategy)

Example: to show the use of questioning to prompt deeper thinking about vocabulary

- Have I ever seen this word before? How was it used? What other words could mean the same? (Modeling and thinking aloud)

Collaborative use and guided practice

Depending on the needs of the students, the teacher can adjust the amount of support given in independent, partner, and small-group tasks that ensure repeated exposure to new vocabulary. The following section illustrates opportunities that can be used in collaboration with the students or for guided practice. Each activity aims to provide students with opportunities to engage with new words and to develop a metacognitive awareness about what to do when faced with an unfamiliar word.

Independent, partner, and group activities

The activities below are preceded by suggested learning goals, as described in chapter 1, that you can adapt and share with the students before they start an activity.

Create opportunities for students to explain *what* they are learning, *why* it is important, and *how* they have used their learning. These opportunities can be found before, during, and after the activities are used. By explaining to each other and to others, students develop a metacognitive understanding of vocabulary-building strategies.

Teachers can also encourage and assist students to take the learning goals and develop possible success criteria for an activity. For example, they can use the stem "We will know we've achieved this when we can …" to prompt thinking about what they are trying to achieve.

See page 22 for more information about learning goals and success criteria.

Previewing text

We are learning to:

- preview vocabulary we might find challenging before we read a new text
- talk about and code words we might find challenging.

Prior to the reading lesson, identify possible vocabulary challenges in a text. List these for the students to preview and explain the reason for doing this. The students preview the list by thinking about their own knowledge of these words. They code the words according to how well they know them, for example, placing a cross next to words they definitely don't know, a circle for words they are not really sure of, or a smiley face for a word they know. The students refer to their preview during the reading comprehension lesson and again at the end of lesson, making notes as appropriate.

Once students have had experience with the preview strategy, they can preview the text themselves using their own coding. Students identify the words they definitely do not know and the words they are not really sure of. Ask the students to share their lists with you prior to the first reading of the text: the lists may form the basis of a mini-lesson or group discussion prior to reading. The lists are also referred to during the reading comprehension lesson and can be used as the basis for vocabulary study in response to reading.

Predicting vocabulary

We are learning to:

- link to our prior knowledge to predict vocabulary that we think may be found within the text
- use our knowledge of synonyms, definitions, text structure signal words, and other clues to review vocabulary within the text.

Tell students the topic and the type of text structure used in the text. For example, "This text is an explanation about trout fishing." Equipped with this knowledge, students predict some of the vocabulary the author may have used. In the example used, the students might predict *river*, *fishing rod*, *reel*, and *hooks*. As the reading proceeds, the students check their predictions and identify other words and phrases that convey similar concepts. For example, where the student might have predicted *river*, they may find that the author also used the related words *riverbed* and *river mouth*.

Teaching about context clues

We are learning to:

- recognize when meaning can and cannot be found from context
- use other information when we can't use context to figure out word meanings.

Some context clues enable students to easily infer the meaning of a word, others provide clues but are not enough on their own (for example, "I know that *exasperated* is an angry emotion, but from the context, I can't be sure exactly what it means.") while others provide no assistance or may even misguide the reader. Show students that they may need to use more than one strategy to find the meaning of a word.

Consider the following examples:

> *It is like unwrapping a gift, opening the bag at lunchtime. Even after I've used the bag all week and it's limber as a dishrag, I still like opening it and taking out that jelly sandwich.*

> from *Just Juice* by Karen Hesse, **1998**

If students did not know the word *limber*, they could use the context to form a mental image of a paper lunch bag that had been used all week. They could use the simile of a dishrag to figure out that the bag is probably very soft and floppy. Students may be familiar with the word in a different context: *limber* means supple or flexible in relation to physical fitness. Work collaboratively with the students to figure out the best meaning, including checking in a dictionary. Together, you can apply the dictionary definitions to the context to find the best fit. You could also discuss the author's interesting use of simile to describe the lunch bag.

> *In recent times, people have learned how to make use of electricity to produce heat and light and to power all kinds of machines and appliances, from watches to small cars.*
>
> from *Switched On* by John Bonallack, Skyrider* Investigations

Students could use the context as well as their general knowledge to figure out the meaning of *appliances*. The discussion could be extended to consider contexts where it would or would not be applied. You can also use the think-aloud instructional strategy (encouraging students to think aloud too) to help explain why a context clue is or is not useful in figuring out a word.

Developing an understanding of prefixes

We are learning to:

- recognize commonly occurring prefixes
- use our knowledge of prefixes to figure out the meanings of words
- figure out the meaning of a word by examining its parts (morphological analysis).

Commonly used prefixes include *un-, re-, in-, im-, ir-, il-, dis-, en-, em-, over-, mis-, sub-, pre-, inter-,* and various research has cited the benefits of deliberately teaching these to students (Baumann, et al., 2004; Graves, et al., 2002; White, et al., 1989).

Deliberate teaching of these prefixes means explaining a target prefix with its meaning and modeling its use. Involve students in discussion and practice of the target prefix, and show them what to do when they come to an unknown word that starts with the prefix.

For example, when we come to a word starting with a prefix, we:

- think about what the prefix means
- find the root word and think about what that means
- combine our knowledge of the meaning of the prefix and the meaning of the root word to help us know the meaning of the new word
- reread the sentence checking that we have the correct meaning of the word by asking "Does this make sense?"

Have students model and discuss this strategy and encourage them to actively seek out words that begin with a prefix.

Additional activities can include:

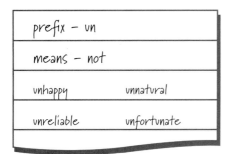

- developing a chart of common prefixes with words that start with each prefix
- developing a poster of common prefixes
- compiling a puzzle or crossword of prefixes for students to complete
- developing a study of root words.

See Appendix 3.1 (page 106) for a list of commonly used prefixes.

Developing an understanding of suffixes

We are learning to:

- recognize the two main functions of commonly occurring suffixes
- use our knowledge of suffixes to figure out the meanings of words
- figure out the meaning of a word by examining its parts (morphological analysis).

In a similar way to the study of prefixes, you can carry out a study of suffixes. Alert students to the fact that there are two kinds of suffixes:

- Inflectional suffixes or word endings add information to the word without fundamentally changing it, for example, they may signal a change in tense or number.
- Derivational suffixes change the meaning of the word (for example, by changing an adjective into noun).

Often, the spelling of the root word changes when a suffix is added: students can carry out a separate exploration of this, determining "rules" that govern spelling changes.

Examples, such as those below, can be explored and charted with students.

Inflectional suffixes	Derivational suffixes
Walk — walked (change of tense)	Happy — happiness (adjective to noun)
Penguin — penguins (change to plural)	Sustain — sustainable (verb to adjective)
Run — running (change of tense)	Deliberate — deliberately (verb to adverb)

This exploration may lead the students to discover that a word can have both kinds of suffix, for example *farm + er + s = farmers.*

See Appendix 3.2 (page 107) for a list of commonly used suffixes.

Display new words that have been learned
We are learning to:
- find and learn new vocabulary
- use our new vocabulary often.

Finding new words can become an exciting activity for students and will help to build their motivation and enjoyment of language. Set up a display board on which students can write or display new or unusual words they come across in their reading. Encourage them to monitor and maintain this display. Students can write puzzles or games for others that require knowledge of word meanings. These can be used as a class or group activity or can be set up at as part of a literacy learning center. They are an ideal way of promoting active problem solving around language and its usage.

Use a variety of displays, including word walls, logs, class logs, and mobiles.

Role-play use of vocabulary

We are learning to:

- use new words to show we understand them
- use words we know in different situations.

For this activity, display a list of words that have been generated from a current vocabulary study and present a word and its definition to one pair of students. They either:

- role-play a conversation using the word, or
- role-play an event to which this word is central.

The other students then work in pairs to identify the word from the list.

Using questioning to understand word meanings

We are learning to:

- use new vocabulary in a variety of contexts
- think about the variety of ways a word can be used
- critically discuss words, their meanings, and their usage in different contexts.

This activity involves students in learning to ask and answer questions about a word. The type of questions could include:

- Would you use this word to describe x? Why/why not? (For example, "Would you use "profound" to describe a lake?")
- When would you expect to see this word used?

- In what context would this word be found?
- Could this word be used in this way …?
- How is "dropping" different from "falling"? How is it similar?
- Can you give an appropriate and inappropriate example of this word in context? (For example, "The protesters tried to disrupt the meeting" and "She had to disrupt the chocolate to give everyone a share.")
- In what ways do some words take on different meanings when they are used in a specific context? For example, how does the meaning of "square" change when it's used in math? How does the meaning of "mature" change when it's used in biology?

Word of the day – guess my word

We are learning to:
- think critically and selectively about words and their meanings
- think more widely about how words are used and what they may mean
- engage actively with word learning.

Students take turns to provide a word of the day and give clues for the word as the day unfolds. Other students are challenged to identify the word from the clues. For example, the word for the day is *sufficient*. Clues could be:

- not too much
- not too little
- just enough
- the right amount for the job
- enough food to give everyone some.

Word sorting

We are learning to:
- sort words into categories based on their meaning.

Students sort vocabulary according to set criteria and attributes using a variety of formats, including Venn diagrams, charts, box diagrams, and semantic maps.

Venn diagram

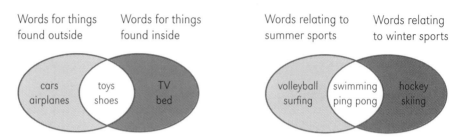

Words for things found outside | Words for things found inside

- cars
- airplanes
- toys
- shoes
- TV
- bed

Words relating to summer sports | Words relating to winter sports

- volleyball
- surfing
- swimming
- ping pong
- hockey
- skiing

T-chart

Words to describe someone who is happy	Words to describe someone who is sad
cheerful	mournful
smiling	upset
radiant	despairing

Chart

For example, chart words that could be used to describe objects, such as rocks in a geology study.

Sample	Feels	Looks	Other properties
A	brittle crumbly	sparkling shiny	abrasive
B	rough	solid black	magnetic
C	soapy hard heavy	dull opaque	

Exploring root words

We are learning to:

- use root words to make other words
- describe how new words relate to words we already know.

Have students engage with word-play activities around the root word. Examples include word webs and word family cards.

Cloze activities

We are learning to:

- use (syntactic and semantic) context clues to figure out the meaning of a word
- talk about our vocabulary choices and explain our choices to others.

Provide the students with a cloze (a passage of text that has the words you wish to focus on deleted). Work with them as they read the passage and try to figure out what the missing words might be. Discuss the context clues to make their decisions. Focus the students on both the syntactic clues (the part of speech that the word would be) and the semantic (meaning) clues to find words that make sense and are grammatically correct. Encourage them to discuss their ideas and provide reasons and evidence for their decisions.

When you eat something, you're _____ air as well as _____ . The air

_____ down your throat and into your _____ with the food.

Categorization

We are learning to:

- make connections between new vocabulary and our prior knowledge.

Give students a list of categories in which to place newly learned words. To do this, they place the new vocabulary into categories that they can connect with their own experiences. They can then explain their decisions to other students. For example, using the word *remarkable*, students can categorize according to:

Remarkable

Person	Time
My Gran Nana	My 12th birthday
Place	**Event**
Redwood forest	Passing my exam! School concert

- person (who is remarkable)
- act (that they felt was remarkable or made them feel remarkable)
- time (that was remarkable or when they felt remarkable)
- place (that they could describe as remarkable)
- event (that they could describe as remarkable).

Any number of categories may be used for this activity with students also providing category headings.

Exploring word derivations

We are learning to:

- recognize Greek (or other) derivations and understand their meanings
- figure out new words by using the Greek (or other) derivations in them
- play with using derivations to make new words.

This activity is best used when the students have already come across words that are derived from Greek (or Latin and other languages). Science is one rich source of words: the names for different kinds of dinosaurs are fun to study.

After introducing the concept that many words come from other languages, encourage the students to keep a list of all the words they find that could have those origins. Discuss the meanings of the word parts and chart them (for example, *auto* = self, *photo* = light, *graphos* = to write, *bios* = life, *logy* = speech or thought, *saurus* = lizard, *tyranno* = tyrant).

(a) Write words that have Greek, Latin, or other derivations on index cards (or in a list) and ask the students to figure out their meanings by using the charts they have made. They can check their work by using a dictionary. Alternatively, they can look up the words in a dictionary and find the meanings of the parts of the words. Examples could include: *quadricycle, hectogram, polylingual, telegram, biosphere.*

(b) Write the derived word parts on cards. The students can put cards together to create new words and suggest meanings for them based on the meanings of the parts.

Words that go together

Many words in English have common associations. Examples include salt and pepper, black and white, hot and cold. Other words are commonly found together, such as red hot, bright and early, ride a bicycle, drive a car. You could initiate a study of these associations as they appear in texts the students are encountering. Knowledge of these associations deepens the students' "knowing" of the individual words.

Classroom talk

Think about the kind of talk that goes on in the classroom. Be mindful of engaging students in regular and cognitively challenging talk about words. This includes discussion during strategy use and vocabulary activities. Encourage students to describe how new words relate to their own prior experiences. Similarly, model and encourage rich vocabulary in discussions that will bring about lots of vocabulary-rich talk in the classroom.

This can be carried into all areas of school life if all teachers and other staff are encouraged to use rich vocabulary. Teachers could spend a few minutes in every regular grade-level or school-wide meeting to discuss the kinds of words that they could focus on in the coming week. For example, teachers could decide to use as many variations on "good" as possible. Students could try to guess the focus word for the week and collect examples of alternatives for the word.

Reading to students

Students of all ages acquire much new vocabulary from having lots of exposure to text. In particular, when teachers read aloud in the "read to" or shared reading approaches, they provide opportunities for students to interact with sophisticated vocabulary that they may not otherwise meet. Reading aloud to students is also an excellent way to introduce words in subject areas such as science, social studies, or math. In doing so, select texts to meet student need and provide challenges and give prereading instruction that anticipates new or unfamiliar words. As you read, identify key words, interesting words that the author has used, unusual turns of phrases, idiomatic usage, or words that may have multiple meanings. Provide an explanation for words that the students do not know, recording them for later follow-up.

For good readers, many new words are learned through incidental learning and from reading a lot of texts. Oral language has a large and important role to play too, and this can be developed through rich classroom discussions and what Pressley, Disney, and Anderson (2006, page 223) call "high-quality curricular events."

When readers struggle

The following are suggested areas of instruction for students who struggle with learning vocabulary. As with all of the examples this chapter has provided, you will need to monitor their effectiveness and modify the instruction accordingly.

There are many reasons why some students acquire a larger vocabulary than others. These may include:

- the amount of exposure students have had to text (being read to as well as independent reading)
- the amount of exposure students have had to rich and varied vocabulary
- the students' proficiency in noticing, understanding, expanding, and remembering new word meanings
- their familiarity with English (in particular, the idiomatic, figurative, and colloquial use of English) if this is not their home language.

Students who struggle with vocabulary are less likely to retain new words as they read and are usually less likely to read extensively. For these students, opportunities for deliberate and intentional vocabulary improvement need to be planned, regular, sustained, and carefully monitored within the regular classroom reading program.

For all students (whether they struggle or not), daily vocabulary instruction is best where teachers endeavor to move instruction beyond "telling" students to demonstrating, explaining, discussing, making their thinking explicit, and involving students in supported practice.

The article we're reading today has a piece about a system to help people read in the dark. The article contains a word I'd like to explore with you so we can look at strategies for understanding new words.

Louis Braille

Our best ideas often stem from something we'd like to improve in our own lives. Thinking about how to solve a problem has led people to create some of the most amazing inventions in the world today. Louis Braille made a huge difference to the lives of blind people all over the world. He left his mark—six of them in fact—by inventing a system of reading and writing for the blind, using six raised dots in different patterns.

Louis Braille was born in 1809 in a small town outside Paris, France. He lost his sight when he was just 3 years old in an accident in his father's workshop. Louis was lucky enough to be offered a scholarship to the Royal Institution for Blind Youth in Paris when he was 10, but the students were expected to learn everything by listening to their teachers speak out loud. The school library had fourteen books that had raised letters of the alphabet, but these were difficult to read and complicated to produce. When Louis was 12, a former soldier visited the school and told the students about a system of "night writing" that soldiers had used to communicate in the dark—a code of twelve raised dots. The system hadn't worked because the soldiers had found it too difficult, but this didn't **deter** Louis. He worked hard to improve the system, using half as many dots to make it easier to follow.

from "Making a Difference" by Rebecca Green, Power Zone* *Leaving Your Mark*

(The teacher writes the sentence on the whiteboard: "The system hadn't worked because the soldiers had found it too difficult, but this didn't deter Louis.")

I came across the word deter, and I wasn't sure what it meant. I thought I could pronounce it OK – de/ter.

I reread the sentence. I checked the words around deter and found two clues: the words but and didn't – "but this didn't deter Louis." These words told me that maybe Louis didn't think it was too hard and that he wouldn't give up. This was confirmed in the next sentence. Putting all this together, I reasoned that deter meant stop, prevent, or put off. The fact that the system hadn't worked didn't put Louis off trying again. Can you think of a time when a problem or difficulty didn't deter you from doing something?

The following section provides some suggestions for supporting struggling students to learn new vocabulary. It is not, however, intended to be an exhaustive list and should be considered in conjunction with the examples given earlier in this chapter. Students who struggle with vocabulary benefit from sustained instruction through which they build an in-depth understanding of how words can be used, which can be easily overlooked. As with the activities above, sharing the learning goals and creating opportunities for students to explain what they are learning will help to develop a metacognitive awareness of their own learning processes.

Choosing the vocabulary focus

Because students who struggle need multiple encounters with new vocabulary to retain the new words, working with words should be considered a long-term activity.

Select, preteach, teach, follow-up

Review texts that students will be reading during shared, guided, and other instructional approaches, as well as those they need to read in specific subject areas. Identify the words that they are likely to find difficult. These are the words to preteach and they should mostly be tier 2 words (see page 78).

Each word chosen for instruction should be a word that the students will encounter again, be one that relates to an area the group is studying, or be central to understanding the main idea in the text. This is an opportunity to teach students how to make connections between the new word and their own knowledge. By making clear the similarities between the focus words and words that the students already know, you can reinforce the learning.

As the students come across the word, demonstrate one or two specific strategies that they can use to figure out its meaning. In this way, you scaffold the learning: the students have already been told about the word and what it means. Now they can try a variety of strategies to test and confirm the meaning, and you can demonstrate how the strategy can be applied in their own reading.

After reading, include a vocabulary activity that develops from the lesson and provides continued practice of new vocabulary.

List challenging words

It's important to build your awareness of the vocabulary that students are likely to find difficult. As a reading lesson progresses, keep a record of words that students find challenging by writing them on a whiteboard or chart. These words can then form the basis of vocabulary learning.

Regular instruction

Provide regular instruction on strategies to figure out unknown vocabulary. This involves teaching students when and how context can be used to figure out the meaning of new words, when morphemic analysis (breaking a word into parts) is most suitable, and when to combine both context and morphemic approaches.

Using context involves looking for clues within the text to figure out the word. Sometimes the definition is in the sentence or surrounding sentences, sometimes a synonym or antonym is present, or an example may be given. Teach students to look for these clues as they read.

Using morphemic or structural analysis involves examining the parts of the word – the suffix, prefix, root word, compound words – to figure out the meaning.

Developing student knowledge of synonyms is an effective way of linking a new word to a concept already familiar to a student.

New Word	Synonym
liable	likely ("Liable to happen," "likely to happen")
anticipate	expect, prepare, get ready for, be prepared for, wait to happen

Similarly, students can chart synonyms and antonyms for a new word – again if these are based on a word the student already knows, then it helps to embed the new vocabulary.

New Word	Synonym	Antonym
reasonable	Not bad, good enough, rational, make sense	Unreasonable, awful, irrational

Assist students to see a new word used in different contexts. Use graphic organizers to build on knowledge of new vocabulary that is based on a main idea, concept, or event in text.

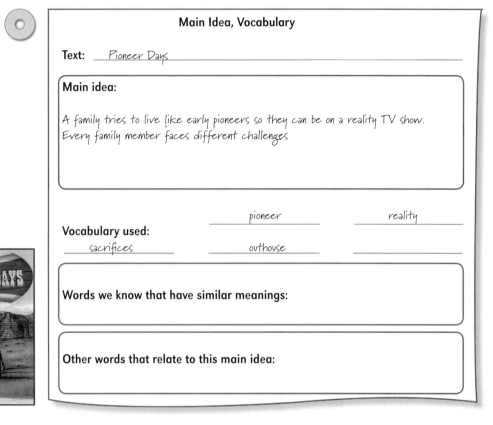

Main Idea, Vocabulary

Text: _Pioneer Days_

Main idea:

A family tries to live like early pioneers so they can be on a reality TV show. Every family member faces different challenges

Vocabulary used:

	pioneer	reality
sacrifices	outhouse	

Words we know that have similar meanings:

Other words that relate to this main idea:

from *Pioneer Days* by Susan Paris, Skyrider* Investigations

Using reference materials

Students who struggle with vocabulary may need extra support with using reference tools. This includes teaching them how to use a glossary, a thesaurus, and a dictionary. Electronic as well as print-based materials can be used, and games and puzzles can help students gain confidence with these tools so they can access them independently. Part of this instruction will need to focus on selecting the best meaning when there are several in a thesaurus or dictionary.

Keep motivation in mind: students who struggle will benefit from instruction that builds curiosity and interest in words. A teacher who loves words and uses them eloquently and playfully can transmit this interest to students.

Time for vocabulary instruction

Having a time specifically set aside for vocabulary learning each day is essential for all students. Students who struggle may need an extra five to ten minutes of well-planned vocabulary instruction in addition to the pre- and post-reading activities. In cross-curricula instruction, time spent teaching new vocabulary is important for all students and may need to be extended for some. Deliberate time spent on vocabulary instruction will not only improve overall vocabulary but will increase students' reading comprehension.

It is always important to provide lots of time for independent reading of text at appropriate levels and for all students to read to one another. Researchers, for example Anderson (1996) and Stahl (1998), believe that increasing the amount of reading students do is one of the best ways of increasing their vocabulary.

Extending able readers

For the more able students, vocabulary instruction will be aimed at developing deeper or broader inquiries into how and why words are used. At the same time, provide support as they engage in the new vocabulary. The following suggestions show how you can increase the opportunities for extending the more able readers in a class.

- With the students, spend time (as part of prereading activities) learning the subject-specific vocabulary they will encounter in the text, encouraging them to predict the meaning of these words. Encourage use of a wide variety of strategies and word sources to support new word learning. Have the students make connections between the new subject-specific vocabulary and the words and concepts they already know (for example, by using a graphic organizer) and provide opportunities for new words to be used orally and in context.
- Attend to academic vocabulary needs – these are words that are used in an education context and that students will encounter in English, math, science, history, social studies, and technology. Many will be tier 2 words if they are used frequently. Academic word lists can be found on the Internet (for example, see http://www.vuw.ac.nz/lals/research/awl/index.html).

- Allow time for students to develop group learning around the "word of the day" notion. Encourage them to share interesting words they have encountered; words used in technical, picturesque, and unusual ways; and words that allow for punning or other word plays.
- Students may benefit from selecting and teaching words to their peers. This could include preteaching of vocabulary specific to a class topic. Students could select the strategies to present the new vocabulary to their peers based on strategies that have been developed in class.
- Encourage wide and extensive reading to enable vocabulary development to continue to grow.
- Involve students in investigations of vocabulary. This could include:
  - investigating the origins of words and word families (Greek and Latin derivatives are excellent examples.)
  - exploring language used for particular purposes, for example, vocabulary used in advertising
  - exploring language used for particular audiences, for example, by comparing how the purpose of language remains the same but the form changes (how the word choice changes if you are talking to an adult, a teacher, a peer, a younger student, a police officer, a minister, a school principal, or a brother)
  - comparing the regional differences in words, for example, clothing for swimming can be called a swim suit, swimming togs, bathers, swimmers, costumes, cossies, or boardies
  - developing a study of homonyms.
- Allow students to decide their own topics for study. Students may present their studies in a variety of ways, including PowerPoint, visual display, and 3D display.
- Focus on words with multiple meanings. Involve students in active investigation and discussion of these words. Encourage them to actively look for these words and how they are used. For example, *ease* can mean:
  - to do something with ease – easily
  - to ease off on a piece of work – stop, let it go, take the pressure off
  - to slide and push something away.
- Build and extend vocabulary through discussion and role-playing.

- Encourage students to explore vocabulary through talk.
- As part of pre- and post-reading activities, encourage students to create vocabulary puzzles for one another. (For example, crosswords with clues from the text; "guess the word" where clues are given one at a time for other group members to decipher – this could include saying what a word looks like and what it does, giving a synonym or an antonym, the part of speech it is, or where it is commonly used)
- Explore language in different literary genres such as fairy tales, poetry, science fiction, fantasy, and historical fiction. Students could carry out a study based on the works of a particular author such as Jean Little, C. S. Lewis, Jane Yolen, J. K. Rowling, Gary Paulsen, or other authors who have written series of stories.
- Students can use drama as a way of exploring idiomatic language, for example, by writing expressions on word cards that must be used in a role-play.
- Use new, complex, and challenging vocabulary with students to scaffold use of words and provide opportunities for them to explore new words.

Developing metacognitive awareness

All of the activities described above encourage students to develop a metacognitive awareness of the strategies that they can use to increase their reading vocabulary. By using metacognitive comprehension instruction (see chapter 1), teachers can take every opportunity to develop students' awareness of what they are learning. This happens through high-quality dialogue between teacher and students, and between students.

As students practice the strategies, teachers encourage them to record what they are learning, what they are finding difficult, and why. They can do this in a variety of ways, for example:

When I come to a word I don't know the meaning of, I can:

look for clues within the text
- definitions
- examples
- synonyms
- other clues

look at the structure of the word
- recognize prefixes and their meanings
- recognize root words and their meanings
- recognize suffixes and their meanings.

Name: Gerry   **Date:** 2/19/07

I am learning to:

use root words to figure out the meanings of new words

What I did:

Summary

Researchers (Biemiller and Slonim, 2001; Pressley et al., 2006) stress the need for deliberate, high-quality vocabulary instruction at all grade levels. This chapter has looked at the ways teachers can gather information on the vocabulary needs of their students and use this to provide deliberately planned vocabulary instruction. Vocabulary instruction has a strong relationship to reading comprehension. This can be strengthened by linking instruction to the students' prior knowledge and by planning instruction to be challenging and metacognitive. Ensuring that all students have a repertoire of strategies to advance their vocabulary knowledge is an essential part of reading comprehension instruction.

References and recommended reading

Anderson, R. C. (1996). "Research Foundations to Support Wide Reading." In *Promoting Reading in Developing Countries*, ed. V. Greaney. Newark, Delaware: International Reading Association, pp. 55–77.

Baumann, J. F. and Kame'enui, E. J. ed. (2004). *Vocabulary Instruction: Research to Practice*. New York, New York: The Guilford Press.

Beck, I. L., McKeown, M. G., and Kucan, L. (2002). *Bringing Words to Life: Robust Vocabulary Instruction*. New York, New York: Guilford Press.

Biemiller, A., and Slonim, N. (2001). "Estimating Root Word Vocabulary Growth in Normative and Advantaged Populations: Evidence for a Common Sequence of Vocabulary Acquisition". *Journal of Educational Psychology*, 93, pp. 498–520.

Blachowicz, C. L. Z. and Fisher, P. J. L. (2000). "Vocabulary Instruction". In *Handbook of Reading Research Volume III*, ed. M. L. Kamil, P. B. Mosenthal, P. D. Pearson, and R. Barr. Mahwah, New Jersey: Erlbaum, pp. 503–523.

Blachowicz, C. L. Z. and Fisher, P. (2002). (2nd ed.). *Teaching Vocabulary in All Classrooms*. Englewood Cliffs, New Jersey: Merrill/Prentice-Hall.

Blachowicz, C. L. Z. and Fisher, P. J. L. (2004). "Vocabulary Lessons". *Educational Leadership*, 61(6), pp. 66–69.

Blachowicz, C. L. Z., Fisher, P. J. L., Ogle, D, and Watts-Taffe, S. (2006). "Theory and Research into Practice Vocabulary: Questions From the Classroom". *Reading Research Quarterly*, 41(4), pp. 524–539.

Elley, W. B. and Smith, J (1997). *How Children Learn to Read: Insights from the New Zealand Experience*. Auckland, New Zealand: Longman.

Graves, M. F. (2006). *The Vocabulary Book: Learning and Instruction*. Newark, Delaware: International Reading Association.

Graves, M. F. and Watts-Taffe, S. M. (2002). "The Place of Word Consciousness in a Research-based Vocabulary Program." In *What Research Has to Say about Reading Instruction*, ed. S. J. Samuels and A. E. Farstrup (3rd ed.). Newark, Delaware: International Reading Association, pp. 140–165.

Greaney. V. (1996). ed. *Promoting Reading in Developing Countries*. Newark, Delaware: International Reading Association.

Hynd. C. R. (1998). ed. *Learning from Text across Conceptual Domains*. Mahwah, New Jersey: Erlbaum.

Marzano, R. J. (2004). *Building Background Knowledge for Academic Achievement: Research on What Works in Schools*. Alexandria, Virginia: Association for Supervision and Curriculum Development.

McKeown, M. G. and Beck, I. L. (2004). "Direct and Rich Vocabulary Instruction". In *Vocabulary Instruction: Research to Practice*. ed. J. F. Baumann and E. J. Kame'enui. New York, New York: The Guilford Press, pp. 13–27.

Nagy, W. E. (2005). "Why Vocabulary Instruction Needs to Be Long-term and Comprehensive". In *Teaching and Learning Vocabulary: Bringing Research to Practice*, ed. E. Hiebert and M. L. Kamil. Mahwah, New Jersey: Erlbaum, pp. 27–44.

Nagy, W. E. and Scott, J. A. (2000). "Vocabulary Processes". In *Handbook of Reading Research*, vol 3, ed. M. L. Kamil, P. B. Pearson, and R. Barr. Mahwah, New Jersey: Erlbaum. pp. 269–284.

Nation, I. S. P. (1996). ed. (revised ed.). *Vocabulary Lists*. Wellington: Victoria University English Language Institute.

National Reading Panel (2000). *Report of the National Reading Panel.* Washington, DC: Government Printing Office. www.nationalreadingpanel.org

Pressley, M., Disney, L., and Anderson, K. (2006). "Vocabulary". In *Reading Instruction that Works: The Case for Balanced Teaching.* M. Pressley (3rd ed.) New York, New York: The Guilford Press, pp. 220–239.

RAND Reading Study Group. (2001). *Reading for Understanding: Toward a Research and Development Program in Reading Comprehension.* Santa Monica, California: RAND Education.

Samuels, S. J. and Farstrup, A. E. (2002). ed. *What Research Has to Say about Reading Instruction* (3rd ed). Newark, Delaware: International Reading Association.

Stahl, S. A. (1998). "Four Questions About Vocabulary Knowledge and Reading and Some Answers". In *Learning from Text across Conceptual Domains*, ed. C. R. Hynd. Mahwah, New Jersey: Erlbaum, pp. 73–94.

White, T. G., Sowell, J., and Yanagihara, A. (1989). "Teaching Elementary Students to Use Word-bit Clues". *The Reading Teacher*, 42.

APPENDIX 3.1

Prefixes

Prefix	Meaning	Examples
a-	toward, near	aside, along, away
dis-	not, the opposite of	disagree, discover, disappear
im-	not, the opposite of	impatient, impossible, imperfect
in-	not, the opposite of	incorrect, independent, insignificant
inter-	between	international, Internet, intersection
ir-	not, the opposite of	irresponsible, irregular, irrelevant
mid-	middle	midair, midfield, midnight
mis-	wrong	misbehave, misfortune, mistake
non-	not	nonfiction, nonsense, nonstop
over-	above, too much	overalls, overdue
pre-	before	premature, prepacked, preteen
re-	again, back	recycle, replay, rewrite
sub-	under, part of	submarine, subtitle, subway
super-	more than, above	superbug, superhuman, supersonic
tele-	far away	telegraph, television
trans-	across	transform, transatlantic
un-	not, the opposite of	undo, unlucky, unreal
under-	below	undercover, underground
uni-	one	unicycle, uniform, universe

APPENDIX 3.2

Suffixes

Suffix	Meaning	Examples
-able or -ible	able or can do	fashionable, horrible, comfortable
-al	relating to	natural, accidental, personal
-ary	like, connected with	dictionary, imaginary
-en	made from or make	frozen, wooden, frighten
-er	one who does something, more	teacher, computer, greater, faster
-est	most	largest, oldest, funniest
-ful	full of	beautiful, careful, helpful
-ish	like	foolish, selfish
-less	not, the opposite of	speechless, careless, lifeless
-ly	like	quickly, suddenly, nearly
-ment	result of	development, argument, excitement
-ness	describes being	happiness, kindness, illness
-ous	connected with	dangerous, poisonous, furious
-sion, -tion	expresses an action or state	explosion, decision, pollution, collection
-th	result of	growth, depth, health
-y	inclined to	thirsty, muddy, sleepy

Reading with Fluency

This chapter discusses the important relationship between fluency and reading comprehension, and it explores how fluency instruction can be integrated into classroom reading instruction and cross-curricula instruction in grades 3 to 8. While fluency instruction is necessary for all students, some students require more or varied instruction according to their particular needs.

Key messages for teachers

- Fluency and accuracy of reading affect a student's overall comprehension and ability to make meaning from text.

- Fluency is an important part of becoming a strategic and proficient reader.

- The critical test of students' fluency is their ability to decode a text and comprehend it at the same time.

- Reading comprehension instruction can teach behaviors associated with fluent and accurate reading.

- There are strong links to decoding and word recognition. To increase fluency, students must learn to recognize words accurately and automatically (automaticity), rather than with accurate and deliberate word recognition that is not fluent (see also chapter 2).

- Automaticity develops through extensive practice at reading a wide variety of texts at instructional and independent levels, including the rereading of familiar texts, especially for those who may be reading at an emergent or early reading level. Automaticity must be accompanied by comprehension.

- Fluency also involves prosodic features: reading with appropriate pace (rate of reading), phrasing (also known as chunking of text), intonation (use of stress and pitch), and loudness.

- Teachers can deliberately assist students to read with greater fluency and accuracy. Developing fluency is an important part of instructional reading and of reading across the curriculum.

- When students are actively involved in their own learning, they are more likely to develop metacognitive understandings about fluency and how it affects comprehension.

Reading fluency refers to the reader's ability to develop control over surface-level text processing so that he or she can focus on understanding the deeper levels of meaning embedded in the text.

Rasinski, 2004, page 46

The diagram below shows the various aspects of reading fluency and how they work together to support comprehension. Note that not all aspects have equal "weight" – for example, accuracy and automaticity are more important than speed.

Reading Fluency

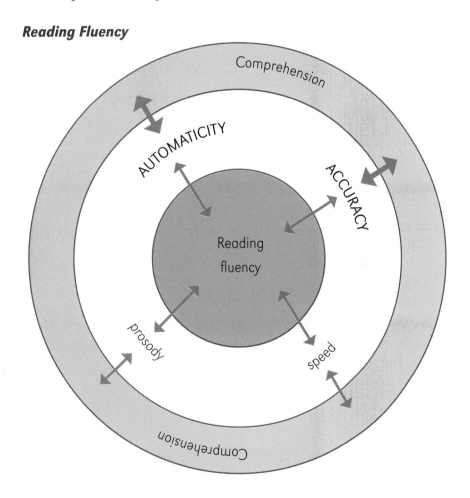

Identifying student needs

As discussed in chapter 1, teachers collect data about the strengths and needs of their students before they decide what to teach. The data will also help them to determine the best way of teaching the knowledge and skills that their students need.

Different forms of assessment can enable the teacher to determine whether the students are aware of how they are reading, how well they control their own thinking while they read, and how well they understand their reading. As teachers assess the students' fluency, they are able to determine which aspects require additional teaching, and they can incorporate these into their instructional program. Two methods for finding out about students' fluency are targeted observations and teacher–student interviews.

Targeted observations

Teachers can plan to observe students as they read. Teacher-made checklists or anecdotal records can be used to record data, based around the following questions:

- Is the student reading with comprehension?
- What is the rate of reading? Is it at a consistent level? Does this vary as the student reads? If so when and why? Can the student explain how and why the rate of reading varies?
- Is their rate of reading affecting overall comprehension – is it too fast or too slow? (If the student is reading very slowly, consider whether this is also the case in silent reading.)
- Does the student read with intonation?
- Does the student read with phrasing – is the student chunking up the text into meaningful segments?
- If so, are these behaviors enhancing comprehension?
- If not, are these behaviors indicating other difficulties such as not automatically recognizing words?

While the student is reading, the teacher makes notes.

After the student has finished reading, the teacher will ask the student to recall what he or she has read to assess the following:

- Is the student able to recall the general overall theme or characteristics of the text?
- Is the student able to recall specific details?

The teacher can question the student about specific details that appear to have been missed and record the responses.

Teacher–student interview

As described on page 20, a planned interview between a teacher and student can give valuable insights into a student's performance and how the student regards his or her own reading. An interview focused on fluency could include questions such as the following:

- What do you think a fluent reader does?
- Do you think that you're a fluent reader? How do you know? What are some of the things you do that fluent readers do?
- Do you ever find it difficult to read a text fluently? What kind of text? In these cases, how do you know that it's difficult?
- When you're reading aloud, does it sound the same as when you're reading silently? How does it differ?
- What do you think an accurate reader does? How do you know? What do you do that accurate readers do?
- What makes reading accurately difficult for you? Can you give me an example?
- How do you know when you are not reading accurately?
- When you don't understand a passage, what affect does this have on your fluency and accuracy?

The information gathered and recorded from one or both of these methods will give the teacher information to guide instruction.

Metacognitive comprehension instruction

Drawing on information from assessment, teachers can plan the instructional activities for their classroom program. Fluency instruction can be incorporated into many subject areas: it need not be limited to literacy texts.

Using instructional strategies and approaches

Teachers can use the instructional strategies, practices, and approaches described in chapter 1 and chapter 6. In particular, modeling, explanation, and guided practice all support independent practice of fluency.

Modeling of fluent reading

Teachers have many opportunities to model fluent reading. In addition to resources in the reading program, teachers can use other content including math problems, directions for science experiments, explanations of scientific or mathematical processes, and excerpts from original documents in social studies. When teachers read aloud texts that the students can see (for example, by using an enlarged text or individual copies in shared reading), they can encourage the students to read along silently or "whisper read." This can lead to teacher and student discussions of fluent reading behaviors.

Examples of teacher modeling:

- *I can see there's an exclamation mark at the end of this sentence, so I'll use my voice to show enthusiasm or excitement.*

- *The long sentences in this scientific explanation can be tricky, but I'll slow down a bit and use the punctuation to decide where to pause and how to phrase it so I can connect the ideas in each sentence.*

Teachers can demonstrate and teach fluent, accurate reading behaviors and explain how these behaviors assist with overall comprehension. Record these for future reference.

Students can also gain valuable practice and feedback from reading aloud to one another. This can be done either in pairs or in small groups. The students who are listening provide the readers with feedback on their fluency, and the students who are reading can reflect on their own learning. The students can be shown this process by teacher modeling first (including appropriate use of focused feedback). They can then be encouraged to describe:

- the behaviors that have assisted them to read with greater fluency and accuracy
- the reader's behaviors that demonstrated fluency and accuracy
- what they have learned from reading aloud and from listening to others read.

See the suggestions for partner reading on page 117 for examples of the behaviors that can be modeled and described.

What do fluent readers do?

Fluent readers:

Read accurately

Know what to do if they need help with a word they do not recognize

Read the text as it would be spoken, paying attention to:

- punctuation
- speed
- tone
- the natural breaks or places where the text can be split into chunks
- the most important words that need emphasis
- the sound of the text so it seems the writer is talking to us

Understand and can talk about what they have read.

Deliberately teaching the behaviors of a fluent reader

Teachers can help students to recognize the characteristics of fluent reading by modeling it themselves and by using the think-aloud strategy to explain what they are doing and why. In addition, students can model these behaviors during the group lessons. There are many opportunities for practicing fluent reading aloud as part of regular group instruction. As teachers and students model and discuss what they are doing, they can develop a group chart (see example on left) of what reading fluently involves. The chart can be referred to during group instruction, during independent group work, and when students are engaged in other reading across the curriculum. Students can also learn to carry out self- and peer assessment using the behaviors listed on the chart.

Repeated oral reading with feedback and guidance

Repeated reading with adult assistance leads to increased fluency more rapidly than repeated reading by the student alone. This is because the adult can ensure that the text is at the correct level, with just enough challenge, and can help to promote both fluency and comprehension.

Therefore, each of the first two options below rely on a teacher listening to the reader and providing feedback. Where another adult is available and can be trained to readily recognize the characteristics of fluent reading, they can also provide this support. Option 3 can be done in a group setting, with an added emphasis on comprehension or vocabulary as required. (Note that these options differ from "round robin" reading in important ways: the students have already experienced reading the text, the students are being assessed by the teacher while the others are engaged in reading for themselves or are engaged in an assigned task.)

Option 1

In small groups, students participate in a repeat reading of a text they have already encountered (for example, in shared or guided reading). The teacher listens to one student reading aloud as others read to themselves. The teacher provides feedback to the reader on specific fluency behaviors. The teacher then listens to the next reader.

Option 2

Students participate in a reading comprehension task while the teacher takes one student at a time aside to listen to him or her read. The teacher provides feedback on fluency behaviors and assists the reader to set a goal for the next reading.

Option 3

The teacher scaffolds a group in a repeated reading task. Students participate in the repeated reading either through choral reading (see page 119) or echo reading (where the students listen to a skilled reader then echo or imitate the reading) and complete the assigned tasks. Students take turns at leading this activity.

Even up here, I could hear the honking of car horns on the street below. I stood looking down at the rush-hour traffic and the people hurrying along the sidewalk.

By that evening, Mom and Dad had finished arranging the furniture. Everything looked cramped in the small apartment: the bookshelf was jammed in beside the sofa and we had to breathe in to squeeze past the dining room table.

"Hmm ..." Mom frowned. "Maybe we'll have to buy some new furniture."

"I think it's cosy," said Dad. "By the way, Mrs. Krause from 12C just gave us a cake. She seems very friendly. In fact, everyone seems very friendly. I guess that's a bonus of living in

> Let's read the page aloud together.

> Now you can take turns to read it. Think about using appropriate tone and pitch, especially for the speech sections.

> Which words show how the characters were feeling when they spoke? We'll list these words for our group discussion later.

> Read the next page together.

> You'll notice that the characters are showing different feelings. What clues does the author give about this?

> Take turns at reading the sentences and phrases these clues are in. As you read, think about how the author intended them to be read.

from *Blackout* by Rebecca Green, Skyrider* Investigations

Independent, partner, and group activities

The activities that are described below are preceded by suggested learning goals, as described in chapter 1.

Create opportunities for students to explain *what* they are learning, *why* it is important, and *how* they have used their learning as they develop fluency. These opportunities can be found before, during, and after the activities are used. By explaining their learning, students develop a metacognitive understanding of the strategies they use to read fluently.

Teachers can also encourage students to develop success criteria for the learning goals. For example, they can use the stem "We will know we've achieved this when we can …" to prompt thinking about what they are trying to achieve.

The fishbowl method (described on page 227) is an excellent way to help students learn about observing and giving feedback on reading behaviors. It can be used as students learn to carry out the following activities.

Partner reading for fluency
We are learning to:
- practice reading fluently by … (the teacher and the students determine the focus, for example, "reading all the words correctly" or "using the punctuation")
- listen actively as our partner reads
- give and receive feedback about the use of fluency behaviors.

Identify the fluency behaviors that your data has shown each student needs to focus on. In pairs, one student reads a familiar text to a partner, paying particular attention to the focus fluency behavior. The partner becomes an active listener who, in addition to listening for meaning, is listening to provide feedback on the focus fluency.

When the first reader has completed the reading and received feedback, the second reader begins.

Feedback can be provided through listening records, monitoring sheets that identify individual fluency goals, or through checklists of behaviors.

In this way, a student can read a section of text several times, developing fluency.

Prepare multiple copies of the Partner Reading Form. These can be laminated for reuse. Show the students how to use the form and, if necessary, role-play a reading session to ensure they understand what to do.

Learning goals could include:
I am learning to vary my voice as I read.
I am learning to use the punctuation and the meaning to help me read with expression.
I am learning to chunk long sentences so I can read them fluently.

Reading with audio support

We are learning to:

- read and listen to a lot of different texts
- copy expressive reading to help us comprehend as we read
- read accurately, with good expression and pace.

This activity provides readers with a sense of how fluent reading sounds and enables them to practice fluency by reading along with audio support.

Give the students access to an audio version of a text (for example, tape, CD, CD-ROM, podcast) and print copies of the text. The audio versions can be compiled using fluent reading by adults or by other students. (Podcasts by schools taken from the Internet may provide examples with age-appropriate voices and topics and could lead to an exchange of material with other students.) The students listen to the audio, then they listen again, reading along with the audio. This can be repeated several times. For an additional focus on comprehension, the audio can include some prerecorded questions or problems at the end of the reading.

Many educational publishers offer professional audio versions of texts using one or more formats. These can provide an excellent resource for this activity.

Other approaches and opportunities

Choral reading

During choral reading, the group reads in unison as they practice particular aspects of fluent reading. The texts should be varied in both their complexity and type. To gain best value for fluency practice, examples should include fiction and nonfiction as well as examples of poetry, dialogue, persuasion, and explanation. Choral reading is also an excellent way for a group to explore a text and its language features.

Sustained silent reading

Sustained silent reading is useful in developing fluency because it provides extended opportunities for students to read a variety of texts. For this opportunity to be maximized however, the texts must be monitored to ensure that they are within the students' independent reading ability. This means that there should be no more than one in twenty words that the student is unable to recognize. If the text is too difficult, the benefits of reading are lost.

Readers' theater

In readers' theater, students recreate the text as a script. They then present the script orally. There are no scenes, actions, or props, only "voices" that are assigned to different readers. The emphasis is on the voice – the tone, pace, pausing, and intonation ensuring that the audience can visualize the setting and comprehend the actions.

Students read and discuss the text. They are then assigned to read character or narrator parts. (If poems are assigned, students may read alternating lines, groups of lines, or verses.) After individual practice, the students practice reading their parts aloud, working through difficult words to improve fluency and expression and to develop their comprehension. Comprehension can be improved when students read to emphasize the most important messages and when they use their own experiences to convey how characters would express themselves. These two aspects of expressive reading are well-supported through readers' theater.

Readers' theater also has the advantage that it can be adapted and that students can select appropriate texts themselves.

Suitable scripts are those that:
- can be read aloud easily
- are written in a format (for example, an enlarged text) that will allow students to look up without losing their place
- contain a lot of dialogue
- contain action and/or suspense
- involve several characters
- incorporate a variety of text types, including traditional and folk tales, poetry, picture books, recreations of historical events, and informational books with lists.

Independent reading

Provide lots of opportunity for students to practice "in the head" fluent reading. This means reading to themselves, but reading with a consciousness of accuracy, attending to changing punctuation, tone, and stress, and developing an awareness of how expression changes throughout the reading. Teachers can discuss and model this, using the think-aloud strategy where necessary. They can also encourage students to share how they read the text to themselves, perhaps pausing to let excerpts be read aloud for others to listen to.

For example, the teacher can think aloud to point out aspects of fluency:
- When I was reading this to myself, I knew to pause because …
- In this part, I knew to use an angry voice in my head because of the exclamation mark and the word "furious."

When readers struggle

The following areas for instruction can be used with students who struggle to read fluently. As with all of the activities in this chapter, the teacher will need to monitor the effectiveness of the teaching and modify the instruction accordingly.

Reading aloud with an audio text

As a further development of the audio activity above, develop a resource of audio versions of texts that include commercial recordings and recordings that students have made (perhaps as a follow-up reading activity and to practice their own fluent reading). As students listen to the audio versions, they should be encouraged to "whisper read" then read aloud from their own copy of the text. This is also recommended as a partner and group activity. Partners can take turns at whisper reading and reading aloud.

Reading along to commercially prepared CD-ROMs

There is a wide variety of these available for schools. They are most effective when students are interested in the topic and text style used by the author (or combinations of styles), so consider allowing students to be involved in selecting the CD-ROMs. Most electronic storybook formats have a "read aloud" function that allows the student to turn the audio on or off at the word, sentence, paragraph, or whole text level. This provides a model of fluent reading and can be used flexibly to provide decreasing support as the student gains confidence in reading the text fluently.

Sustained opportunities for repeated reading

Repeated reading has long been espoused as effective in supporting readers towards fluent oral reading behaviors (Samuels, 1979, 2002; Dowhower, 1989, 1994). Teachers can provide regular and extended opportunities for repeated readings of known texts.

Using shared reading

Shared reading (Holdaway, 1979; Brown, 2004) is a teaching approach where an enlarged text may be read several times, each time for a different purpose. During the first reading, the teacher reads the text while the students follow and listen to the reading. The students may join in. There can be two or three subsequent readings that have a focus on comprehension and where students read parts or all of the text aloud, along with the teacher. As they read aloud, the students have the opportunity to demonstrate and practice fluent reading. Shared reading is best for readers who struggle when it is done in small groups (five to six students). Students can also reread the text in pairs to practice fluency (see also chapter 7 and references).

Other considerations

When students struggle to read fluently, teachers must make deliberate links to phonemic awareness skills and to the students' knowledge of high-frequency words (words that they will encounter frequently in their everyday reading, see page 78). It is likely that fluency will be affected for students who struggle in either or both of these areas.

Teachers need to be very specific with goal setting. Ideally, teachers focus on just one or two main goals, written very clearly in "kid friendly" language with the students. Teachers and students work together to find and provide pathways to achieving the goals. The student needs to be involved regularly in checking progress toward the goal, through self-assessment and through targeted feedback that is specific and includes the next steps required for development.

Extending able readers

When identifying the fluency and accuracy needs of able readers, teachers can pay particular attention to the assessment information. Teachers will need to ask: "Does my data show any aspects of fluency or accuracy that need to be addressed within the instructional program?"

For those students who do have areas of need, individual, targeted goals and supportive activities can be integrated into their daily instructional program. Teachers should also consider how the more fluent and accurate readers use their knowledge and expertise when they are reading a wide variety of texts (fiction and nonfiction) and when they read for a variety of purposes. Reading with fluency and accuracy requires the student to be flexible, adaptable, and in tune with the audience and the author.

Examples of possible fluency goals for able readers might include:

- My fluency goal is to focus on varying the tone of my reading to reflect the author's purpose.
- My goal is to use a louder voice when I read for an audience.
- My goal is to use expression and tone to evoke a particular response from my audience.
- My goal is to speed up my reading without losing the meaning. (This goal relates to silent reading.)
- My goal is to slow down my reading to make sure I'm getting the meaning. (This goal relates to silent reading.)

For many able readers, a focus on fluency and accuracy becomes a lesser part of their instructional program, allowing greater time to be spent on other aspects of comprehension. However, the use of teaching approaches such as choral reading and readers' theater with this group can reinforce comprehension, as well as providing experience with identifying the mood, setting, and purpose.

Developing metacognitive awareness

All of the activities described above encourage students to develop a metacognitive awareness. By modeling fluent reading whenever a text is read aloud and by using metacognitive comprehension instruction (see chapter 1), teachers can develop students' awareness of what they are learning about fluency. This happens most readily through high-quality dialogue between teacher and students, and among students.

When students take over the responsibility for monitoring how fluent they are, they are able to develop metacognitive awareness of their own understandings about fluency, and they can provide support in the form of feedback and advice to one another.

Peer and self assessments provide excellent opportunities for readers to give and receive this kind of support. Additionally, to be able to provide a peer with feedback on his or her performance, the partner needs to pay extra close attention to how the peer is reading. This re-emphasizes the characteristics of a fluent reader.

I listened to you read today, and
I noticed

_____

_____

_____

_____

Signed

My fluent reading goals:

To read without stopping after
each word

To vary my voice to fit in with the
punctuation

To vary the speed of my reading

Goal

To practice stressing the most
important words

To do this, I will_____

_____

I know I will have achieved this
when _____

Summary

The relationship between fluency and comprehension is reciprocal
and develops over time. Learning to become a fluent reader is just one
important dimension of learning to comprehend text. The focus is on
both word recognition and prosody. The transition from accurate and
deliberate word recognition to accurate and automatic word recognition
comes as a result of practice. The prosodic features (which include
intonation and loudness) of oral reading also require exposure to fluent
reading, as well as repeated opportunities for practice. So too with the
development of the self-confidence that being able to read text with
fluency gives the reader. Practice helps to put all the pieces together.
The goal in all reading instruction is increasing student control of
comprehension: the way the teacher organizes and balances the reading
comprehension instruction enables this practice to occur.

References and recommended reading

Brown, S. (2004). *Shared Reading for Grades 3 and Beyond: Working It Out Together*. Wellington, New Zealand: Learning Media.

Dowhower, S. L. (1989). "Repeated Reading: Research into Practice". *The Reading Teacher*, 42. pp. 502–507.

Dowhower, S. L. (1994). "Repeated Reading Revisited: Research into Practice". *Reading & Writing Quarterly*, 10 (4). pp. 343–358.

Harris, T. L. and Hodges, R. E. (1995). *The Literacy Dictionary: The Vocabulary of Reading and Writing*. Newark, Delaware: International Reading Association.

Hasbrouck, J. E. and Tindal, G. (1992). "Curriculum-based Oral Reading Fluency Norms for Students in Grades 2 through 5". *Teaching Exceptional Children*, Spring. pp. 41–44.

Holdaway, D. (1979). *The Foundations of Literacy*. Exeter, New Hampshire: Heinemann.

Kuhn, M. (2004). "Helping Students Become Accurate, Expressive Readers: Fluency Instruction for Small Groups". *The Reading Teacher*, 58(4), pp. 338–344.

Pikulski, J. J. and Chard, D. J. (2005). "Fluency: Bridge Between Decoding and Reading Comprehension". *The Reading Teacher*, 58(6), pp. 510–519.

Pressley, M., with Fingeret, L. (2006). "Fluency". In *Reading Instruction That Works: The Case for Balanced Teaching*. (3rd ed.), M. Pressley. New York, New York: The Guilford Press, pp. 195–219.

Rasinski, T. V. (2000). "Speed Does Matter in Reading". *The Reading Teacher*, 54(2), pp. 146–151.

Rasinski, T. V. (2003). *The Fluent Reader*. New York, New York: Scholastic.

Rasinski, T. (2004). "Creating Fluent Readers". *Educational Leadership*, vol. 61 (6), p. 46.

Samuels, S. J. (1997). "The Method of Repeated Readings". *The Reading Teacher*, 50. pp. 376–381. (Original work published 1979).

Samuels, S. J. (2002). "Reading Fluency: Its Development and Assessment". In *What Research Has to Say About Reading Instruction*. (3rd ed.) A. E. Farstrup and S. J. Samuels. Newark, Delaware: International Reading Association, pp. 166–183.

Working with Comprehension Strategies

This chapter explores ways that metacognitive comprehension instruction can be integrated into general classroom instruction in grades 3 to 8. It provides guidance for teaching that focuses on explicit instruction of strategies to promote students' comprehension. It shows how comprehension strategies are taught in conjunction with other knowledge, skills, and strategies related to decoding and word recognition (chapter 2), vocabulary (chapter 3), and fluency and accuracy (chapter 4).

The chapter explains how teachers can take a strategic approach to developing comprehension. It draws on a substantial body of research that includes the work of Pressley and colleagues (for example, Pressley 1998, 2002, 2006; Duffy, 2003; Dowhower, 1999).

Key messages for teachers

- Effective readers learn to make use of a number of comprehension strategies as they process text.
- These strategies facilitate readers' memory and understanding of text.
- Strategies can be used intentionally, or they can be used without the reader's conscious attention. The key feature of a strategy is that it is controllable: metacognitively aware readers are able to control when and how they select and use strategies.
- Strategies are used by effective readers before, during, and after reading.
- Effective readers can monitor and adjust their reading comprehension and use strategies when required.
- Effective teaching means taking a strategic approach to reading comprehension by providing specific comprehension lessons to build students' knowledge and use of strategies.

- Direct and intentional instruction is effective in promoting reading comprehension.
- When students are actively involved in their own learning, they are more likely to develop metacognitive understandings about when, why, and how to use comprehension strategies.

Comprehension strategies

A readers' use of comprehension strategies can be likened to a tool that readers control in order to assist meaning.

Pressley, 2002

Comprehension strategies are specific, learned procedures that foster active, competent, self-regulated, and intentional reading.

Trabasso and Bouchard, 2002

See also the information about metacognition in chapter 1.

The comprehension strategies discussed in this chapter are:

1. Deliberately making connections to prior knowledge
2. Predicting and re-predicting
3. Visualizing
4. Inferring
5. Self-questioning
6. Seeking clarification
7. Summarizing
8. Identifying main idea
9. Analyzing and synthesizing
10. Evaluating

Effective comprehenders are active and strategic as they read. They use a wide variety of strategies to develop meaning from text. Strategies are not usually applied in isolation: it is through using these strategies in combination that a reader is able to develop meaning. To enable students to become independent users of comprehension strategies, and to do so deliberately when meaning breaks down, the strategies are taught both independently and in combination.

Strategy instruction is about teaching students to be cognitively active as they read, to know when they are reading with understanding, and to know what to do when they are not.

Identifying student needs

While comprehension strategy instruction is necessary for all students, some students require more or varied instruction according to their particular needs. The instructional "mix" is based on the needs of the students and is directed toward providing them with the metacognitive knowledge to help them to choose when, where, and how to use the strategies.

Teachers can best collect data about the needs of their students through ongoing observation, questioning, and discussion as students read, write, and talk about texts. The data they gather and analyze will also help them to determine the best way of teaching the strategies.

This section describes two aspects of comprehension strategy knowledge and use that teachers may need to assess to determine the focus of their instruction. The first aspect is students' general knowledge of the use of comprehension strategies. The second aspect is the use of specific strategies.

General awareness and knowledge of comprehension strategy use

Teachers can determine the extent to which students are able to articulate and demonstrate what they know about comprehension strategies.

- Do the students know that proficient readers draw on a variety of comprehension strategies to assist their understanding of text?
- Do they know some of these strategies and not others?
- What do they need to be taught?

Independent assessment tasks

Students can complete the following tasks independently to provide information about their use of comprehension strategies. The first task requires the students to read a passage and record the comprehension strategies that they used as they read it. The second task is more directive, using a verbal survey.

Read and record

- Select a short (up to a page) piece of text that the students can read independently but has enough challenge to require them to apply comprehension strategies. The text can be fiction or informational, and the kinds of strategies used will vary with the kind of text. (For example, a narrative text or a poem may require more inference than a report.)
- Give each student a sheet of paper to record what they do to help them understand the text.
- Tell the students that as they read the text, they are to list all the things they do in their heads to help them understand it.

If students have difficulty with this task (for example, if they write nothing or write notes on the text), prompt them by rewording the direction or by asking them to explain orally. Students may have difficulty because they don't know what they do or they don't know how to explain it. Understanding these difficulties will inform instruction. For example, if students have difficulty articulating their thought processes, teaching will need to focus on modeling and encouraging them to become aware of what they do "in their heads." Metacognitive thinking can be taught, and students can develop the ability to articulate and make decisions about their thinking.

Student survey (Oral)

Read over the survey forms shown here and select the one that is most appropriate. Each one assumes a different degree of knowledge about comprehension strategies. They are intended to be used orally in discussion rather than as checklists. A conversation between a teacher and a student will reveal more useful information than a list that has been checked by a student who may have no real understanding of what the items mean.

Note that the following examples also appear as appendices at the end of this chapter.

131

Oral Student Survey – Example 1

What do you do in your head to help you understand what you read?

> Connect what I'm reading to things I already know

> Guess what's going to come next

> Make a picture in my mind

> Read between the lines

> Ask myself questions

> Go back and reread

> Summarize as I'm reading

> Look for the big idea or message

> Use other ways to understand, for example, by recalling the sequence of events or the relationships between characters

Now circle the ones you would like to learn more about to help you understand what you read.

Oral Student Survey – Example 2

Here's a list of some of the comprehension strategies that you can use to help you understand what you read. Circle those that you would like to learn more about.

> Connect what I'm reading to things I already know (making connections)

> Guess what's going to come next (prediction)

> Make a picture in my mind (visualizing)

> Read between the lines (inferring)

> Ask myself questions (self-questioning)

> Go back and reread (seeking clarification)

> Summarize as I'm reading (summarizing)

> Look for the big idea or message (identifying main idea)

> Use other ways to understand, for example, by recalling the sequence of events or the relationships between characters (analyzing and synthesizing)

Oral Student Survey – Example 3

Here's a list of some of the comprehension strategies that readers use to help them understand what they read.

> Connect what I'm reading to things I already know (making connections)

> Guess what's going to come next (predicting)

> Make a picture in my mind (visualizing)

> Read between the lines (inferring)

> Ask myself questions (self-questioning)

> Go back and reread (seeking clarification)

> Summarize as I'm reading (summarizing)

> Look for the big idea or message (identifying the main idea)

> Use other ways to understand, for example, by recalling the sequence of events or the relationships between characters (analyzing and synthesizing)

Describe how you use some or all of the strategies on this list. For each strategy you use, tell me:

What the strategy does to help you _____

How you use the strategy _____

When you use the strategy _____

Please list any other strategies that you use and describe how you use them.

Which comprehension strategies are most useful to you as you read? Circle them on the list.

Use of specific comprehension strategies

If you suspect that a student (or a group of students) is not using a particular strategy or is not using it effectively, you can probe the student's use of the strategy to determine the degree of instruction. The two assessment procedures that are described below probe for the use of prior knowledge and of visualizing. The procedures can be used for other comprehension strategies, with the substitution of appropriate questions and prompts.

Informal discussions

Introduce the focus strategy to your students. In this example, the strategy is making connections to prior knowledge. You could use the following questions and promts:

- One of the strategies that readers use is making connections to things they already know. What does that mean to you? (Do not prompt.)
- How do you think you could use this to help you understand a text?
- Tell me where you linked to things you already knew to better understand the text that we read this week.

If students are unable to answer these questions, you may prompt by telling them what making connections to prior knowledge means.

- Making connections to things you already know means thinking about what you know and using that knowledge to help you understand what you are reading.

Now repeat the three previous questions.

As you analyze the students' responses, think about:

- When you have clarified the strategy, do the students recognize that this is something that they already do when they are reading?
- How well are the students able to explain their use of this strategy?

Text-based task

You may suspect that some students are not able to use a particular strategy, for example to visualize (get a picture in their minds) as they read. You may suspect this because they are often unable to retell a description in detail. When they do retell, it is brief and they do not use the text to support their ideas.

To find out if your suspicion is correct, you can set an independent task that requires the students to use the strategy.

Select a short (up to a page) piece of text that the students read independently. The text can be fiction or informational, but it should require the reader to use the target strategy. (For example, if visualizing is the target, the text should contain rich description.)

Write a set of questions for the students to respond to as they read, or ask the questions orally. The example below is probing the use of visualizing.

"It's the biggest animal in the world, yet its outer ear is only the size of a pencil tip. Its mouth is so big that thirty people could stand on its tongue, yet it has no teeth. It lives in the ocean, but the blue whale – like other whales – is not a fish. Whales don't have gills like fish do. Instead, they breathe air through blowholes. When a whale comes up to breathe, the blowhole opens so it can snort out stale air and take in fresh air. A blue whale has two blowholes. When it spouts, the water from its breath can shoot up to 30 feet in the air – that's as high as a three-story building."

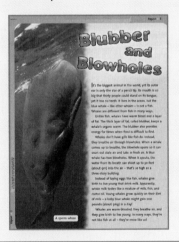

> *Based on what you've read, what can you tell me about the size of a blue whale?*

> *What words or phrases has the author used to help you form a picture in your mind of blue whales?*

> *Which are the most important clues? Why do you think they are important?*

from *Blubber and Blowholes* by Helen Frances, Write Tools

As you analyze students' responses, think about:
- To what extent do their responses indicate that they have a good understanding of blue whales?
- Were they able to identify supportive evidence from the text?
- How did the author's comparisons help them to visualize?

Metacognitive comprehension instruction

As described in chapter 1, researchers suggest that comprehension strategy instruction begins with the teacher modeling and explaining a single strategy. Once students are coping well with this, and are beginning to use it independently, teachers add another strategy so that over time students develop a repertoire of strategies. In doing so, teachers will be aware that it will take time to introduce such a repertoire, and it will take time for students to be able to use them automatically. Teaching is aimed at equipping students with strategies so they know what they are, they know how to draw on them and when to do so, and how the strategies will assist them to comprehend texts.

Opportunities for strategy instruction most commonly occur during small-group instructional lessons – in particular through guided reading and shared reading. However, opportunities also arise where teachers read aloud to their students, through whole-class shared reading, in reciprocal reading, read-along sessions, and paired reading. These approaches are discussed in chapter 6.

Learning goals

Learning goals arise from the needs of students and provide a learning focus for each lesson. They are shared with students at the beginning of each lesson, referred to as the lesson progresses, and used to support self-assessment, peer assessment, and future goal setting. They also provide a basis for discussion and feedback between students, and between students and teachers. As teachers and students become more comfortable with using learning goals, the students (with teacher support initially) can determine what counts as success for these goals and use them as they give self, peer, and group feedback (see pages 22–23 for more information about success criteria and feedback).

When sharing learning goals that are focused on individual comprehension strategies, it is important to remember that strategies are not used in isolation. Learning goals may reflect this depending on the focus of instruction.

Metacognitive comprehension instruction (see chapter 1) allows for a flexible but carefully applied range of instructional practices. It will typically involve a high degree of teacher participation through modeling, questioning, and explaining when a new strategy is introduced.

As students become more proficient at applying the strategy (or a combination of strategies), they can do so in small groups, in pairs, and eventually, independently.

The following section discusses ways to monitor for comprehension: students can learn to do this themselves as they read.

See chapters 6 and 7 for more detailed information about instructional approaches and working with groups.

Monitoring for comprehension

Teachers and students need to have ways of checking that students are understanding texts as they read and that they are using comprehension strategies. Students do this by learning to monitor their understanding as they read; teachers do it by using ongoing observations and discussions.

Students who have been taught to be metacognitive are far more likely to be aware of when they are losing meaning and to be able to call on strategies to fix up their understanding. Direct instruction and activities that allow students to practice self-monitoring can help sharpen this process.

Self-monitoring and fixing up

Self-monitoring is the process by which readers become aware of the characteristics and messages of the texts they are reading, and whether they are understanding them. Readers also learn to determine whether they found the text easy or difficult and why. As they monitor their reading, students learn to detect any problems, to decide whether these problems are affecting their understanding, and to apply some strategies to fix the problems. They will need to use a repertoire of strategies to do this. These strategies will include word recognition and vocabulary, as well as comprehension strategies.

Building student awareness of the importance of self-monitoring and their knowledge of how to fix up their understanding is an important part of metacognitive comprehension instruction. It must be revisited and emphasized throughout a student's reading comprehension development. As students become more proficient at knowing and using a variety of strategies, and learn to draw on them independently, their confidence and ability to fix up faulty comprehension will improve.

Fixing up faulty understanding involves knowing what to do when you don't understand what you are reading. Even expert adult readers do this, and students can be taught to do the same. The activities described here can be used with students individually, in pairs, and in small groups.

Suggested learning goals

We are learning to:

- recognize when we've lost the meaning as we read
- use a variety of strategies to help us fix up problems when we don't understand what we are reading.

Supporting activities

Write learning goals that match the students' needs, then select one or more activities to share with the students. Explain the activity, and if possible, work with the students to write success criteria for self-monitoring and fixing up comprehension problems.

Rereading

Deliberately encourage students to reread the parts that don't make sense and teach them this through modeling (for example, during read aloud and shared reading) and providing opportunities for collaborative and guided practice. Students can try out this strategy in pairs giving each other feedback according to the agreed success criteria.

Sharing strategies

Provide regular opportunities for students to share and reflect on their reading strategies. This can be done as the group completes a section of text or at the end of the reading, or both.

Encourage students to talk about the strategies that helped them figure out meaning when the reading was becoming difficult. It is a good idea to record these as one additional way of developing students' metacognitive awareness. This can also be done in small groups or pairs with one student recording. For example:

- Today when we read, we …
- As I read this text, I used the following strategies to help me understand …
- In this piece of text, I used … strategies. Over here, I used the … strategy.
- I got a bit stuck here, but I knew I would be able to figure out what the author meant by …

Question the students and encourage opportunities to develop peer questioning. For example, by asking:

- *When you read this text, did anyone reread a section in order to understand it better?*
- *What strategy did you find most helpful? Why?*
- *How was this different from the time that we read …?*

Charting strategies

Actively involve the students in drawing up a list of the strategies that readers use to make meaning of text. This list should be compiled by the students to ensure that they have ownership and understanding of it and should be added to as the instruction continues.

At the end of the lesson, the students can refer to the list to review and identify the combination of strategies. Encourage the students to compare the strategies used by the group.

A list of comprehension strategies can also be made into a bookmark. On one side, the students can list the comprehension strategies that they can use, and on the other, they can list words they did not recognize or did not know.

The list below shows some of the items that could be taken from a class chart and written on a student bookmark. It is important to remember that the content and style of these bookmarks will vary depending on each student's knowledge and use of comprehension strategies and the teaching focus.

I can:
- make a picture in my head
- read the confusing section slowly in my head
- ask myself questions and look for answers in the text

When we are reading a text and we lose the meaning or become confused, we can:
• stop and reread up to the point where we were stuck
• think – What do we know already? What are the main points the author has made?
• make a mental picture
• read the confusing section slowly
• think about what the author might be saying
• concentrate and try to get a picture as we read this part
• look for the most important event or piece of information in this section
• ask ourselves questions and look for the answers in the text
• look to see if the author expects us to infer – Are there any clues to help us think through exactly what the author means?

Provide many opportunities for students to practice comprehension strategies in small groups, encouraging them to use the think-aloud approach to explain what they are comprehending and why.

Teacher monitoring of comprehension strategy development

When teachers are sharing lesson learning goals with students, they are able to monitor directly the progress the students are making and the degree of independence and understanding they are developing. During the lesson, and at the lesson's conclusion, the teacher can make brief notes about how each student has participated and the degree of confidence they are gaining for using a specific strategy, or combination of strategies. By asking students to self-assess and to set targets for future lessons, teachers gain further insight that will assist with the instructional decisions they need to make. Teachers can regularly monitor against learning goals and can involve students in this process.

If teachers wish to take student involvement a step further, they can have the students help to develop success criteria to match the learning goals for an activity. (See page 23 for more information about success criteria.)

For example, if students are learning about the comprehension strategy of summarizing, the lessons will have focused on identifying the main events within text. The learning goals and success criteria developed and shared with the students could include:

Strategy focus
Summarizing information from the text

Learning goal
We are learning to identify the most important ideas as we read.

Success criteria
We will be successful when we can:

- pick out the key sentence
- highlight the key words and justify why we chose them.

At the conclusion of each lesson, the teacher and students discuss the progress made, and the students use a code to monitor their progress.

- I managed really well with this today.
- I am getting better at this.
- I am just starting to understand this.
- I need lots more help.

Encouraging critical awareness

Comprehension also involves the development of critical thinking about texts. As they read and listen to texts of all kinds, it is important to draw students' attention to the social and cultural perspectives conveyed through the text. Students will need to consider this as they articulate the author's point of view and purpose, reflecting critically on the themes, the information sources, and the style. The development of critical awareness becomes a part of every comprehension strategy. In particular, it can be explored as students learn to use the strategies of inferring, self-questioning, identifying the main idea, analyzing and synthesizing, and evaluating.

Teaching comprehension strategies

This section describes ten key comprehension strategies that are used by good readers. Teachers need to use metacognitive comprehension instruction as they introduce the strategies and as they introduce activities that allow the strategies to be practiced.

The examples below take each strategy in turn, describing the strategy then providing examples of possible learning goals relevant to the strategy, as well as several activities that can be used for deliberate instruction. These learning goals and activities are not intended to be a complete or conclusive list.

Deliberately making connections to prior knowledge

Making connections to their prior knowledge, also known as a reader's "schema" (Anderson and Pearson, 1984), is a strategy that readers draw on to help them make sense of new information before, during, and after reading. By connecting to prior knowledge, readers use and adapt their schema as they read and discuss text. This may include adding to their existing schema, making connections to different things in their experience, connecting with things they have read about or seen elsewhere, connecting new knowledge to knowledge they already have, and deleting inaccurate of irrelevant information.

Students can draw on a number of schema. These include:

- their knowledge, beliefs, and understandings about the topic they are reading about
- their knowledge of the kind of text and text structure they are reading
- their cultural knowledge, background, and beliefs
- their world experiences, including emotional experiences
- their knowledge of and beliefs about their own reading abilities and potential barriers to comprehension
- their knowledge of how authors write for different purposes and use styles to suit their purposes and points of view.

Students use all kinds of prior knowledge to check their understanding as they are reading, to assist them as they pose questions of the text, to help them predict what will happen next, to create visual images as they read, and to support them as they synthesize, analyze, and evaluate what they are reading. They can focus on what they did not understand and relate this to their prior knowledge to build comprehension. As students become metacognitive in their learning, they learn to think about and articulate how they have deliberately connected to their prior knowledge to enhance their comprehension. (See page 16 for more information about prior knowledge and schema theory.)

Suggested learning goals

Depending on the needs of the students, the activities that follow could use one or more of these learning goals or they can be used as models for writing more specific learning goals.
We are learning to:

- find ideas (or words, information, events) in the text that we already know and use this to help us understand new ideas in the text
- make connections with what we already know to help us to understand the new information in the text

- identify what we know already about a topic before reading and compare this with what we know after reading – what was similar, what was different, what was new
- make connections between this text and others we've read on this topic (or by this author, in this genre, style ...)

Supporting activities

Write learning goals that match student needs, then select one or more activities to share with the students. Explain the activity, adjusting the support to enable the students to eventually work on it independently.

Brainstorm before reading

Have students brainstorm and record what they already know about the topic, events, genre, or ideas in a text before they read. After reading each section (for example, two or three paragraphs), stop and ask the students to make links between what they already know and what they have read. Ask:

- *How did what you already know help you to understand what you've read?*
- *What more do you understand now about ...?*

Highlight the ideas that students already knew. Use a different colored pen to add the new knowledge they find in the text.

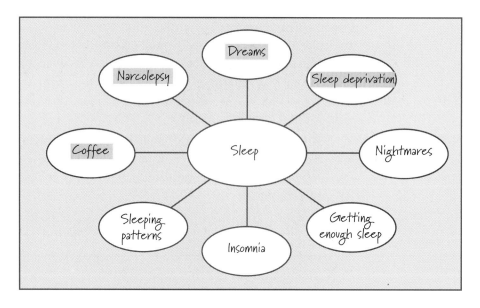

From "Sleep–Who Needs It?" by John Bonallack, Power Zone* *Sleep*

You may also ask students to write concluding statements, for example:

- What I knew before I read this text
- How this helped me to understand the text
- What I know now. (This requires students to synthesize the new information and is an example of using more than one strategy to comprehend a text.)

Skimming

Begin by asking the students to skim a section of text to get a general sense of the content. Remind them that this may include looking at titles, subheadings, illustrations, and the first and last sentence. This activity requires students to make predictions and is an example of using more than one strategy to comprehend a text.

Ask students to discuss their responses to parts of the text.

- *Do these parts remind you of things you already know? What are they?*
- *How do the subheadings help you to predict what's in the section?*
- *Based on the connections you've made, what might you expect to find in this text?*

They can jot down the ideas, events, words, or topics that are already familiar to them.

Reporting back

Provide lots of opportunities for students to report back on the new ideas they have learned and to discuss these in relation to what they knew before. Encourage them to identify how their prior knowledge helps them to make sense of the new ideas.

This activity is particularly useful when you are introducing a topic that is unfamiliar to most students. For example, if you are in a rural area and few students have experienced a big city (or vice versa) you may need to spend some time building prior knowledge. For example, you could make them aware that they can draw on different sources to help them, such as television, movies, and books set in the unfamiliar setting. You could discuss the sounds, smells, and sights that they might expect and help them relate these to things they already know. Students often need to be reminded that they have prior knowledge, even if it is not direct experience. (This activity may involve visualizing as well as linking to prior experience.)

You may like to give the students supports to help with this discussion or to use as prompts as they learn to make links to their prior knowledge. These could be in the form of index cards with headings such as:

- Today I read about …
- This is a little like … that I already knew.
- My knowledge of … helped me to understand …
- Now I also know …

This is a classic example of how comprehension strategies work together. Even if the lesson or activity focus is on linking to prior knowledge, it is worth drawing students' attention to the fact that they are doing many different things at the same time.

Connecting key ideas

When students are reading several texts or chapters on a topic or theme, you can encourage them to make connections between the texts by asking them to examine the key ideas that the texts share. They can then list the connections, giving examples from each text. Use a variety of points for comparison, for example, fiction and nonfiction texts on a related theme, texts that convey different points of view, and texts that use different kinds of vocabulary on a similar topic.

The examples below use simple, well-known fables to highlight the strategy. Replace the examples with more sophisticated texts as soon as the students have understood the purpose of the activity.

Topic or theme: Fables

Text title	Connections
Fox and crow	Foolish and wise pair of characters
Tortoise and hare	Story has a moral

When students have also learned to use the strategies of self-questioning or synthesizing, these can be added to this activity, requiring students to use two or more strategies.

Text title	Connections	A question I have
Fox and crow	Moral	Why do these stories often use talking animals?
Tortoise and hare		

Text title	Connections	Synthesis
Fox and crow	One foolish, one wise character	Using very different characters helps to make the point and convey the moral of the story.
Tortoise and hare		

Starting from the known

The KWL approach, originally developed by Donna Ogle (1986), can be used as a way of activating and connecting to prior knowledge. It provides a structure for accessing and building prior knowledge and guiding students through what they know, what they want to find out, and what they have learned.

KWL: Given your current knowledge of the topic and structure of the text:	
K – what do you already know?	
W – what do you want to find out?	
L – what have you learned?	

This approach can also be modified to include a focus on vocabulary as follows:

KWVL: Given your knowledge of the topic and structure of the text:	
K – what do you already know?	
WV – what vocabulary do you expect to find?	
L – what have you learned – about both content and vocabulary use?	

Predicting and re-predicting

Predicting is the comprehension strategy through which the reader tries to determine future ideas and events before they appear in the text. It is also sometimes referred to as forming and testing hypotheses. Good readers anticipate and predict ahead of time to make educated guesses about what will be in the text. They draw on their prior knowledge to do this (knowledge gained from life, social, and cultural experiences, and knowledge of the topic, the text structure, and the author), making and confirming predictions as they form connections between their prior knowledge and the new information in the text.

Students can be taught to use clues from the text, both before and during reading, to make, verify, and revise predictions. The clues include the cover, title, the subheadings, the illustrations, the glossary, and the cover blurb. Information from these sources can all be used to form predictions. As students read, they test their predictions, monitoring and asking questions as they do so. This will often mean revising their predictions (based on what they have learned from the text so far and from their prior knowledge) to form new predictions. Thus predicting and re-predicting is cyclical or recursive in nature.

Metacognitively active students have learned how to make informed predictions. They know how to read to confirm their predictions, to use their predictions to monitor their understanding of the text, and to revise or make new predictions based on what they have learned. They are able to demonstrate how their use of the predicting and re-predicting comprehension strategy assists them to make meaning of a variety of texts, and they can describe the learning benefits they gain from utilizing this strategy.

Possible learning goals

We are learning to:

- think about the vocabulary the author uses and predict what might happen next based on these vocabulary choices
- predict and read on to check our predictions
- make a prediction and give evidence from our own experience to justify our predictions
- make a prediction and give evidence from the text to justify our predictions
- predict, give reasons to justify our predictions, and read on to check our predictions.

Supporting activities

Write learning goals that match the students' needs, then select one or more activities to share with the students. Explain the activity, adjusting the support to enable them to eventually work on it independently. Provide lots of opportunities for students to practice the strategy in small groups, using the think-aloud approach to explain what they are doing as they use the strategy and how this is helping them to comprehend what they read. You may need to model this at first, giving feedback to guide and support the students as they engage in the activities themselves.

Key words

Provide one or more key words from each section of the text. Students use these words to predict what each section will be about and what they expect to find out. They check and re-predict as the section is read. Similarly, phrases taken from the text can also be used as a basis for predicting.

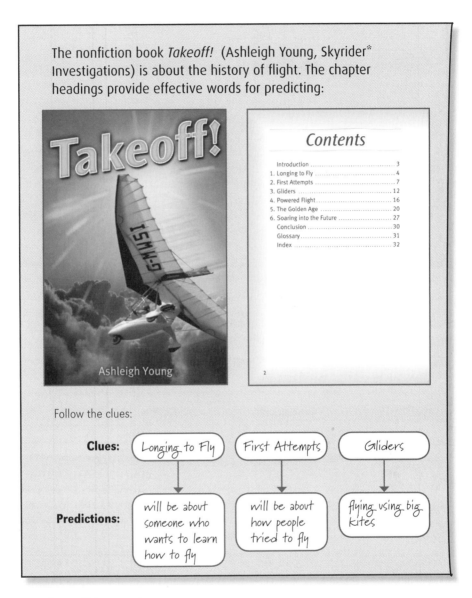

The nonfiction book *Takeoff!* (Ashleigh Young, Skyrider* Investigations) is about the history of flight. The chapter headings provide effective words for predicting:

Contents

Ashleigh Young

Follow the clues:

Clues: Longing to Fly   First Attempts   Gliders

Predictions: will be about someone who wants to learn how to fly   will be about how people tried to fly   flying using big kites

Read, predict, record

As they read, ask the students to pause after each section. The students share and record their predictions, giving evidence to support them. This evidence may come from their prior knowledge or from the vocabulary. It may also come directly from clues in the text or from a combination of these sources.

You can model responses that students could use, for example:

- This phrase supports my prediction because …
- There are three words that support my prediction. They are … and they all relate to …
- I know that when people do …, it usually means …

Clues within text also include the author's use of punctuation (for example, to indicate an emotion), the way sentence structure varies (for example, changing to short sentences to build up anticipation), and the graphics and illustrations.

Prediction cards

Develop a series of cards to record predictions and evidence as the text is processed. These can record the evidence of the predictions or the results from checking the predictions.

Section of text	Prediction	Evidence

Section of text	Prediction	Actual

Critical points

As students are reading, ask them to stop at critical points to identify and share their predictions. You could model starters such as:

- The main thing that is happening now is …
- My prediction for the next section is …
- A question I am asking myself is …
- The prediction I am making is …

Sharing predictions

Encourage students to share their predictions and ask for peer feedback. Peer feedback could come in response to questions such as:

- Do you think I might be correct? Why or why not?
- What important information or ideas have I missed?
- Have I missed any clues?
- What else do I need to think about?

Visualizing

Visualizing is a comprehension strategy used by readers to create a visual image of what they have read. The images can emerge from all five senses, as well as from the feelings and emotions portrayed by the author. Visualizing helps readers to relate to the characters in a story because they can imagine how they feel and what they are like. Through visualizing, students learn to use their senses and their imaginations to help make the text alive and vibrant.

The image created by the reader also helps them to understand and remember what they are reading. The image is influenced by the style of the author's writing and the words, phrases, and techniques used to "paint a picture." As readers visualize, they are linking what they already know about words, descriptive language, and ideas (their prior knowledge) to the messages and main ideas in the text. They can identify words that are descriptive or have led them to forming an image of a character, a process, an event, a place, or a time. The use of this strategy is often likened to "creating a movie in your head." Visualizing is very closely related to inferring because visualizing strengthens the reader's ability to infer.

Students can practice this strategy in small groups, using the think-aloud approach to explain what they are visualizing. They can identify the clues from their senses and the language used by the author to draw them into the text and support their visualizations. They can explain how this strategy (and others used in combination) is helping them to comprehend the text.

Possible learning goals

We are learning to:

- create pictures in our minds as we read and think about what we "see" as we read
- make connections between what we know and the author's message to create an image as we read
- identify key words that help us create a picture in our mind
- identify phrases that build a picture in our mind
- identify structures used by the author to build a picture in our mind
- think about the image created by the text to build our understanding of what we are reading.

Supporting activities

Write learning goals that match student needs, then select one or more activities to share with the students. Explain the activity, adjusting the support to enable the students to eventually work on it independently.

Vivid descriptions

Model this activity using texts that have vivid descriptions. As the students read, prompt them to complete sentences such as:

- The picture I get is … because …
- When I read this, I saw … because …

Sketching

Ask the students to read a section of text (for example, a portion or section from a fictional story, an informational text, or a verse or selected lines from a poem) and then complete a simple sketch of what they have read.

Wild Ideas

They're wild, my ideas.
You can watch them run, but there's no way
you could ride them. I sit on the fence
in my head. I don't dare go near them.
I've tried taking them
by surprise – creeping up, hardly breathing,
till I'm certain
they're not looking. "Is this another
of your wild ideas?" my dad groans, and I know
what he's thinking: wild ideas
won't get you anywhere.
But I'd love to leap
on the back of the wildest one,
squeeze my eyes shut,
and gallop into the unknown.
Where do wild ideas go
when they're galloping home?

Wild Ideas by Ashleigh Young, Skyrider*
Shared Reading Fiction

Alternatively, ask the students to read a section of text, complete a simple sketch or diagram of what they have read, then label it using words (evidence) from the text.

The students can discuss their sketches, explaining how the text guided their drawings.

Charting images

Show the students how to use a chart to record their visual images and the words that helped them to form them.

What do I see, hear, or feel as I read?	Why is this? (words, phrases, structure)

Brainstorming images

Before starting a topic study, develop a group or class brainstorm around a central image, idea, or concept related to the topic. Write the image in the center and ask the students to suggest supporting ideas around it.

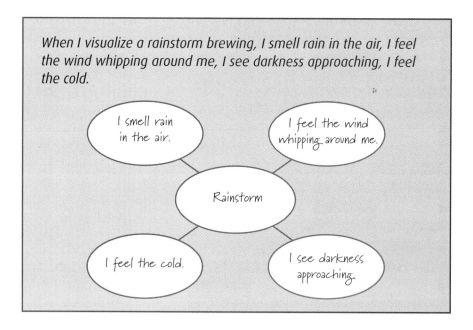

When I visualize a rainstorm brewing, I smell rain in the air, I feel the wind whipping around me, I see darkness approaching, I feel the cold.

I smell rain in the air.

I feel the wind whipping around me.

Rainstorm

I feel the cold.

I see darkness approaching.

As the topic study progresses, have the students find examples of the images they have described in the texts they have read.

Flowcharts and mind maps

Show the students how to develop a flowchart that shows a visual image developing. This can be particularly helpful for showing students how to visualize a sequence of events or an explanation of a process.

From "The Wave" by Norman Bilbrough, Power Zone* *Adrenalin*

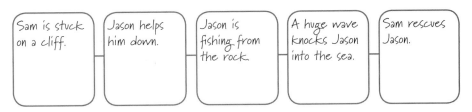

Alternatively, you could use a mind map to show how a process, explanation, event, or description can be visualized. Students can use sketches, words, or phrases to record the images that form in their minds as they read. Remember that visualizing can include senses other than sight – reading a story set in the Arctic in winter can make the reader shiver!

Inferring

Through inferring, students learn to build meaning by using what they already know and the implicit information the author provides. It is based on implied information: information that the author has not stated explicitly.

Inference is based on the reader's prior knowledge, the information they are gaining from the text as they read, their word and vocabulary knowledge, and their ability to draw on information. It involves the reader in making a considered guess about what the author actually means and is very similar to making predictions. Inferring is often referred to as the act of "reading between the lines" where the reader works with the clues the author has provided to gain deeper meaning.

Students using this strategy learn to recognize that meaning may not always be explicit. They learn to search for clues to confirm deeper meaning and to support "hunches" (inferences) they gain as they read. These hunches are implicit ideas based on clues provided by the author and develop as students read and search for understanding. To do this, students draw on their ability to predict what they think the author is stating and then read on to find evidence to confirm their inference. Sometimes readers also need to determine any social, cultural, and political perspectives that may influence their view of the text and the inferences they make. Inferences will be confirmed, altered, or disregarded as readers reflect on their validity and draw conclusions about what an author is saying.

It is important to involve the students in explaining and demonstrating what they did to infer. Have students describe what they did and the thinking behind this (by using the think-aloud approach) while also encouraging them to talk with one another about their awareness of comprehension and their use of comprehension strategies.

Possible learning goals

We are learning to:

- understand the difference between something stated explicitly and something stated implicitly
- read between the lines to understand what's happening in the story, even though the author doesn't tell us directly

- look for clues to identify an author's particular perspective and consider the effect this has on how we comprehend the text
- form predictions based on implied (unstated) meaning in the text
- search for clues the author gives us to add meaning to text and share these clues with others
- use these clues to get a clearer picture of what the author is actually telling us
- make inferences and then change them as needed.

Supporting activities

Write learning goals that match the students' needs, then select one or more activities. Students need explicit instruction that teaches them what inferring means and how they can do it. The following activities give two ways of providing this instruction.

1. Teaching how to infer

Using the think-aloud approach described in chapter 1 (see page 25), you can begin by writing on the whiteboard a sentence where the reader can make an inference. After reading the sentence aloud, discuss the information that the author provides indirectly by looking for clues in the sentence and using prior knowledge. Different colored pens can be used to highlight the author's clues. Demonstrate how the author conveyed the information and how you know this.

Start with a simple sentence and draw out inferences about the setting and the characters:

> "Water dripped off the leaves and landed as puddles on the already sodden ground –"
>
> *I can infer that it is raining, using clues and other strategies:*
>
> > *clues from text: water, dripped, landed, puddles, sodden*
> > *prior knowledge: that rain forms puddles*
> > *visualization: I can see the rain hitting the leaves, bouncing off and splashing on to the ground – there must be a lot of rain to make so many puddles!*

> "The letter was written on thin, yellowing paper and rustled when she unfolded it."
>
> > *I know the letter must be old because the author says the paper is yellowing.*
> >
> > *I worked this out because I know that some kinds of paper go yellow when they're very old.*
> >
> > *The author says the paper rustled. That's something else that tells me it's probably old. I know that thin paper becomes brittle when it's old so it would make a rustling noise when you open it.*

This process can then be extended to several sentences or a paragraph. Students can work on excerpts of text with large sheets of newsprint and colored pens.

Rich questions

Rich questions are those that aim to encourage students to think deeply about text. They require students to think about what they know, to consider the author's purpose and style, and to engage in discussions with others in response to reading. When questions are carefully planned and strategically placed in discussion, they are effective in building students' metacognitive awareness of how and what they are comprehending. *See also chapter 6, page 203, for more information about rich questioning.*

Rich questions, aimed to develop conversation about inferences, include:

- What do you think the author is really trying to tell us?
- What do you think the author means by this?
- How did you figure this out?
- What other strategies assisted you? (for example, prior knowledge, making connections, visualization) How did they assist you?
- What personal viewpoints (mine or the author's) may be influencing the way I interpret this text? How is this so?

2. Literal and inferred meanings

Teaching students what inference is and how to infer also involves focusing them on the difference between literal and inferential messages. After reading a section of text, teachers can use charts to identify those messages actually stated in the text (what I know) and those inferred based on clues in the text (what I feel).

I used an extract from Harry Houdini – Wonderdog! *to help my students to distinguish literal from inferred information.*

What I know	Evidence
he is a dog	use of "dog", "the pound"
he is male	use of "he", "his"
has smelly breath	vet says "Talk about bad breath" when he breaths on her

What I feel	Evidence
a nuisance	the vet thinks Joe is crazy for keeping him, Mom and Dad get frustrated with him
is funny looking	the vet isn't sure if he is a dog or not

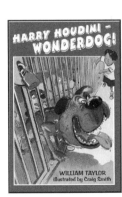

From *Harry Houdini – Wonderdog!* by William Taylor, Skyrider* Chapter Books

Inferences may change as students read on and more information is divulged. In these cases, student learn to reflect on and modify their inferences.

Students need opportunities to practice this strategy with the teacher supporting, modeling, and explaining how they are inferring, as well as practicing with their peers in small groups. Students can use the think-aloud approach to explain what they are inferring, how they are inferring, and what other strategies they are using.

Self-questioning

Self-questioning (sometimes referred to as "questioning" or "questioning the text") is a comprehension strategy where readers ask questions "in their heads" to check that they are understanding what they read. Readers instinctively and purposefully ask questions before, during, and after they read, and they attempt to answer these as they interact with the text.

Self-questioning supports students as they engage with the ideas in the text. This strategy also assists students to monitor their own reading – to recognize when they do not understand what they are reading and to know what to do when this occurs. The questions that readers ask themselves may be:

- directed at particular features of text (for example, information in side bars)
- directed at a particular answer or piece of information within the text
- directed at understanding a particular perspective conveyed by the author
- focused on unusual or new content ideas
- focused on meaning
- to clarify unknown vocabulary – words, phrases, sentences
- focused on structure (for example, sequence, flashbacks)
- aimed at setting a purpose for reading a particular piece of text
- to assist with forming predictions as they speculate on text they have not read

- aimed at uncovering the author's intent, purpose, or position within the writing (for example, does the author's purpose remain consistent or does it change?)
- focused on drawing attention to their metacognitive strategy use (for example, "What other strategies can I use to help me?" "What can I do to understand this section of text better?").

Students who learn to ask questions as they read understand how this will deepen their understanding of text. They learn to determine whether the questions they ask are likely to be answered directly within the text or whether they will need to draw on their prior knowledge to infer the answer. They learn to focus their questions toward the most important information. Sometimes questions are evaluative, helping the reader to make considered and evidenced-based judgments. Asking questions can help the students to evaluate the effectiveness of their questions and to identify the learning benefits from asking and answering questions.

Encouraging students to discuss their questions, to share why they are important to their overall understanding of text, and to share the learning gains made as a result of asking questions are all effective ways of supporting the students to become metacognitively active comprehenders.

Possible learning goals

We are learning to ask questions:
- about particular features of the text
- about new or unusual ideas we do not fully understand
- about the author's purpose and the effect this has on the text
- to help us figure out a challenge we meet in the text
- to help us better understand the text and the author's message
- to help us find specific information in the text
- to extend our understanding beyond the ideas in the text.

Supporting activities

Write learning goals that match the students' needs, then select one or more activities to share with them. Explain the activity, adjusting the support to enable the students to eventually work on it independently.

Bookmarking or charting

This activity requires bookmarks for individual use or chart paper for group use. Explain the learning goal, modeling if necessary. You may wish to add support by providing starters such as:

- A question I have is …
- I'm wondering …

Ask the students to write the learning goal at the top of their bookmark or chart. They can use them to note questions. The students can also note the page number alongside each question. After reading, they can share their questions, discussing whether they were answered in the text. The bookmarks can be used during reading in any part of the day, across content areas.

Using specific questions

Teachers can further support students by teaching them to ask specific questions for different purposes. Initially teachers and students may use the "5W and H" questions (what, why, when, who, where, how) that probe understanding. However, it is also important for students to learn other kinds of questions:

- Literal – these are questions that require students to recall facts directly from the text. When asking these questions, students are learning how to locate the information. *When did Jose leave home? How many times did the spider try to throw the web across?*

- Inferential – these are questions requiring students to think from given clues. Students take the literal information and combine it with other information (in the text and from their prior knowledge). Questions of this type introduce the students to other ways of thinking about the text. *Why did Joshua say he would come home with a surprise? What's the significance of an idea being proven by experiments?*

- Investigative – these are questions that require students to draw conclusions from given clues. Students apply the information to make generalizations, to hypothesize, or to discuss different points of view. *I don't agree with the author that kids are getting lazier – I wonder how you could prove that kids do as much homework now as they did in the 1970s?*

- Evaluative – these questions require students to make judgments based on the text content, the author's style, and the author's purpose. *This story about the 1918 influenza epidemic was scary, but it left me wondering what the author's purpose was in writing it – did she want to scare us into preparing for another epidemic?*

As students learn to question as they read, they learn to connect with the ideas in the text, to explore an idea or aspect that they find confusing, and to probe further to comprehend the author's intent and meaning.

Have students practice the self-questioning strategy in small groups, using the think-aloud approach to explain what they are asking, the behaviors they employ to answer their questions, and how asking and answering questions helped them to gain a better understanding of the text.

Seeking clarification

Seeking clarification is the comprehension strategy where readers seek assistance when they are not sure about something or when they become confused. This will involve students in rereading a section of text, linking what they have read to their prior knowledge and asking questions to clear up their confusion. It may also involve asking another student for assistance, consulting a second source of information (for example, a dictionary, a thesaurus, a website), or seeking assistance from the teacher.

Readers may use this strategy to seek clarification:
- of words they do not know
- of words with multiple meanings
- of phrases that have unfamiliar content or structure, form, or layout
- when concepts are unfamiliar

- when sentence and text structures are difficult to follow
- when a fact doesn't make sense.

In each case, readers who are able to pause and seek clarification before reading further are learning how to monitor their comprehension, are realizing when they are and are not understanding the text, and are taking an active role in developing their own understanding of text.

As readers seek to clarify text, they also learn to explain what they did and demonstrate this to others. Students can use the think-aloud approach to share what they did and why they made their choices when seeking clarification.

Possible learning goals

We are learning to:
- identify the part of the text that we are not sure about
- state what it is that makes us confused
- engage in discussion to seek explanation and clarification
- use reference materials to help us understand a part of text that we do not understand (materials can include websites, dictionaries, encyclopedias, subject guides).

Supporting activities

Students can be taught to be aware when they have lost the meaning as they read and to take steps to clarify their confusion.

Write learning goals that match the students' needs, then select one or more activities to share with them. Explain the activity, adjusting the support to enable the students to eventually work on it independently.

Backtrack and jot

Teach students that when they are confused, they can refer back through the text, jotting down the key things up to the point when they became confused. The notes form the basis for discussion with the teacher and/ or members of the group to clarify unknown material.

Asking questions for clarification

Assisting students to ask clarifying questions encourages them to internalize the clarification strategy. Questions that are useful for promoting clarification include:

- What part of the text is unclear?
- Why am I confused?
- What could this mean? (jot ideas down)
- Which is most probable and why?
- How can I seek assistance?

Develop a prompt chart

Work with a group to develop a chart of their ideas about what they do when they need clarification. Discuss the ideas and write them on the chart for reference. The chart can be copied for pasting into the students' notebooks, displayed for others to refer to, or used as the basis for group members to teach others.

When I need to clarify something as I am reading, I can:

- reread the part of text I need to clarify
- read on to see if I can figure it out
- make connections between this part and the parts that I have already read
- check a dictionary to confirm word meaning
- check a thesaurus
- check an encyclopedia to verify a fact or learn more about an event, a person, or a setting.
- ask an expert.

Develop prompt cards

Provide prompt cards for students to use as they read, both during instructional reading and during independent reading. Discuss the ideas on the cards and teach them how to use them as strategy reminders. As the students become more confident with the clarifying strategy, they can develop prompt cards for others. Examples could include:

- A word I need to clarify here is …
- An idea I need to clarify is …
- I need help with this because …

Group practice

Provide time and opportunities for students to practice using the clarification strategy in small groups. They can use the think-aloud approach to show where they needed clarification, to explain the information in the text, and to show how they drew on their prior knowledge to seek clarification.

Summarizing

Summarizing is the comprehension strategy where students determine what information is important and to combine the key points into succinct statements about what they have read. As students learn to summarize, they learn to construct a brief retell of an entire text. They learn to differentiate between the important information and the supporting details. This includes their ability to determine key words, facts, main ideas, and main events. As they do this, students learn to make decisions about which information to include in their summary and which to discard.

Often readers will draw on their knowledge of text structure to help them summarize. Fiction and nonfiction texts are structured differently, and there are a variety of text structures within each of them. For example, a play is structured differently from a poem and an explanation is structured differently from an argument in a persuasive text. In order to summarize a text, students learn to draw on:

- their knowledge of text structure and organizational features (which may include chapters, headings, and subheadings)
- their ability to identify and interpret the key idea in each paragraph (often but not always found in the first sentence of informational reports)
- their ability to interpret visual supports (for example, graphs, tables, and diagrams)
- their knowledge of the kind of language used within specific text structures (for example, connectives, verbs, proper nouns).

In creating summaries, readers state (either verbally, visually, or in writing) the most important information in their own words. They use language that is clear and precise. They link the information in an organized way that is easy, accessible, and logical.

Possible learning goals

We are learning to:

- identify the structural features of the text
- determine the important details in the text
- combine the ideas
- condense the ideas
- state them in our own words
- order the key ideas to develop a succinct statement, or series of succinct statements, that capture the essence of the text.

Supporting activities

Write learning goals that match the students' needs, then select one or more activities to share with them. Explain the activity, adjusting the support to enable the students to eventually work on it independently.

Highlighting

For this activity, students will need copies of texts that they can write on. The students begin by reading a section of text. On the second reading, they use highlighter pens to locate what they think are the most important ideas. They discuss, justify, and sometimes alter their decisions with their peers.

Next, the students return to the text and record key words that relate to the parts that they have highlighted. Once again they share their ideas and give reasons for the words they have selected. When the section is completed, the students use their key words to develop a statement that summarizes the text.

Finding the key sentence in a paragraph

To assist students to find a key sentence in a paragraph, provide them with the template below to write what they think is the key sentence along with their reasons. This activity can be done as a group, in pairs, or independently. Students share their reasoning, give and seek feedback from others, and decide on the effectiveness of their decisions.

Key sentence selected from paragraph	Reasons for selecting this sentence

Sequence of main ideas or events

This activity is suitable for texts that convey information in a sequence. Texts can include those with a clear and obvious sequence (for example, a procedure, a short biography, or a narrative poem) through to narratives where a story is told with flashbacks or other devices that obscure the sequence.

Each idea is placed in sequence as students make their way through the text. This sequence is later referred to as the students develop a summary of the text.

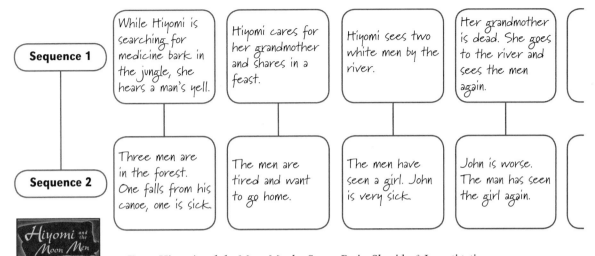

| Sequence 1 | While Hiyomi is searching for medicine bark in the jungle, she hears a man's yell. | Hiyomi cares for her grandmother and shares in a feast. | Hiyomi sees two white men by the river. | Her grandmother is dead. She goes to the river and sees the men again. | |
| Sequence 2 | Three men are in the forest. One falls from his canoe, one is sick. | The men are tired and want to go home. | The men have seen a girl. John is very sick. | John is worse. The man has seen the girl again. | |

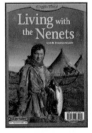

From *Hiyomi and the Moon Men* by Susan Paris, Skyrider* Investigations

Justifying importance

In this activity, students are asked to identify supporting evidence to justify their choice of important ideas. This requires them to decide which ideas are important rather than just interesting.

First, the students practice the summarizing strategy in small groups, using the think-aloud approach to explain what they are doing, how this is helping them to comprehend text, and what other strategies they are using. Next, they justify their summaries by finding evidence in the text that supports them. This can be recorded on a chart:

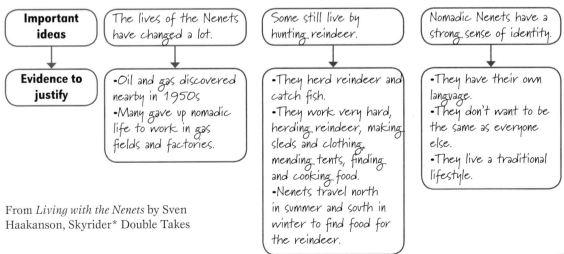

| Important ideas | The lives of the Nenets have changed a lot. | Some still live by hunting reindeer. | Nomadic Nenets have a strong sense of identity. |
| Evidence to justify | •Oil and gas discovered nearby in 1950s
 •Many gave up nomadic life to work in gas fields and factories. | •They herd reindeer and catch fish.
 •They work very hard, herding reindeer, making sleds and clothing, mending tents, finding and cooking food.
 •Nenets travel north in summer and south in winter to find food for the reindeer. | •They have their own language.
 •They don't want to be the same as everyone else.
 •They live a traditional lifestyle. |

From *Living with the Nenets* by Sven Haakanson, Skyrider* Double Takes

Identifying main idea

This comprehension strategy involves the reader in determining the main idea in the text. This is also referred to as the big idea (for example, in a report), the theme (for example, in a narrative text), or the key message (for example, in an argument). Sometimes the main idea is explicit and is revisited and reinforced throughout the text. At other times, it is implicit and the reader has to infer, analyze, synthesize, and evaluate to determine it. The main idea is usually closely related to the author's purpose. On other occasions, thinking critically about the author's reason for writing the text is important in determining the main idea. Additionally, some texts may contain more than one main idea, with some having a greater importance than others.

Students need to differentiate between the topic and the main idea. For example, a text may be about a bicycle race, but the main idea might be about perseverance; a letter might be a letter of complaint, but the main idea might be outrage at injustice.

In order to be able to identify the main idea, students need to learn to:
- interpret what they believe to be the author's purpose
- link to their prior knowledge
- identify any bias or perspectives strongly supported by the author
- make predictions about what the main idea might be
- search for evidence to support their predictions
- infer from implicit information
- synthesize the information
- consider all evidence and make thoughtful decisions
- explain and demonstrate to others how they arrived at the main idea.

Possible learning goals

We are learning to:
- find clues and evidence to help determine the main idea
- combine the clues and evidence and link them to our prior knowledge to determine the main idea
- think about and discuss the main idea that the writer wants us to understand.

Supporting activities

Write learning goals that match the students' needs, then select one or more activities to share with them. Explain the activity, adjusting the support to enable the students to eventually work on it independently.

Events in a narrative

When reading a narrative text (for example, while listening to a novel read aloud), the students can list the main ideas in a chapter or part of the text. For example, for each major event in the story, ask them to identify a possible theme. As the story develops, work with the students to integrate their themes and to determine one overall idea.

Once this strategy has been modeled and the students have had guided practice in using it (for example during read-aloud sessions), they can work in pairs or groups to chart the events and ideas in a novel they are reading, finally arriving at the main idea.

Considering evidence

This activity can be used for fiction but can also be powerful with nonfiction texts on topical issues. As with the previous activity, the students list the main events that occur through the text. They then consider all the evidence and decide on the author's central idea. Students can justify how they figured this out and give reasons for their decisions. The group members provide feedback on one another's reasoning and decisions.

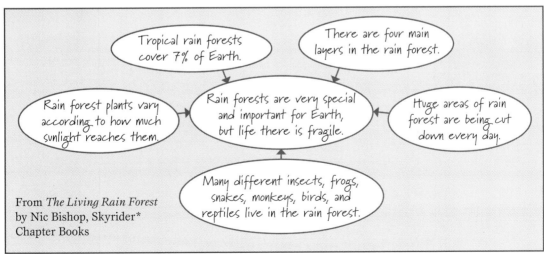

From *The Living Rain Forest* by Nic Bishop, Skyrider* Chapter Books

Where the reader identifies a strong bias within the writing, this activity may also be used to provide evidence for a particular main message. Evidence may come in the form of text style, language, or voice.

Step by step

This activity requires the students to record the processes they went through to figure out the main idea from a text. It can be done independently or in pairs, and the result is shared with the teacher and other group members.

Text title:
1st step: First I …
2nd step: Then I …
3rd step: Next I …
4th step: Then I …
I concluded that the main idea was:

Finding the Main Idea

Text title: The Refugees

1st step: First I read the text through.

2nd step: Then I looked at how frightened the main character was feeling.

3rd step: Next I thought about how the children had to walk to the border of the country.

4th step: Then I tried to think of what had happened to the parents of the children.

I concluded that the main idea was: Because of war, the children have to leave the country, and their parents are lost.

From *The Refugees* by Janice Marriott, Skyrider* Chapter Books

Students can practice this strategy in small groups, using the think-aloud approach to explain what they are doing, how this is assisting them to comprehend the text, what other strategies they are using, and why they are drawing on other comprehension strategies.

Analyzing and synthesizing

Analyzing and synthesizing usually occur together and are part of the process of readers "making the text their own." Analyzing involves students in examining, questioning, and probing the ideas in a text from their own viewpoint. Sometimes particular conditions will affect their ability to analyze – for example their mood, the amount of time they have to read, their level of interest in the topic. Synthesis is about combining new ideas with existing information to form conclusions about the text's meaning.

As students read a text, they learn to stop regularly and think about what they are reading. As they do this, they add new information to their current understanding. They become aware of the changes that are occurring to their understanding and of the conclusions they are drawing from the text.

Combining information and being aware of the changes to their thinking will also help students to monitor their comprehension. Students continue to revise their thinking as they read on, assimilating new information into their evolving ideas about the topic. They examine and probe the new information, synthesizing this with what they already know as they make decisions about a character, a setting, or the overall meaning of the text.

As readers learn to analyze and synthesize they:

- identify ideas and information from within text
- link ideas and information to their prior knowledge and experiences
- compare different ideas and information to create new knowledge
- form summaries and conclusions
- learn to view text critically, including the author's style, perspectives, and language choices
- learn to explain and demonstrate to others how they analyzed and synthesized the ideas and information in a text to assist their comprehension.

Emil and his students had read many different texts about the opening up of the American West. He had chosen texts by writers who had different perspectives, including first-hand accounts. The students had been practicing analyzing the texts by comparing them. Next, he encouraged them to synthesize the information to bring a critical perspective to their reading:

> *We've read and compared several books and articles about the movement of settlers across America.*

> *What do you think were the purposes and points of view of the different writers? What makes you think that? How might this affect the way you read historical texts in the future?*

Provide lots of opportunities for students to practice the strategy in small groups, using the think-aloud approach to explain what they are analyzing and synthesizing and why and what other strategies they are using.

Possible learning goals

We are learning to:

- compare and connect ideas within a text
- compare and connect ideas between two or more texts
- examine the sequence of events and why they occur in the order they do
- question information from the text and form our own conclusions
- read, stop, think, question, and add new information to what we already know
- synthesize to understand more clearly what we have read.

Supporting activities

Write learning goals that match the students' needs, then select one or more activities to share with them. Explain the activity, adjusting the support to enable the students to eventually work on it independently.

Why is it ...?

Select texts that might allow for more than one interpretation or that leave the reader to reach their own conclusions. Reports may provide good examples, in particular those where the author presents conflicting information. Work through some examples with the group before they try to use the strategy independently or in pairs.

Ask the students to make notes under the headings as shown in the example below.

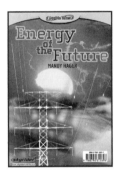

The author states:	Why this could be so	Questions I have are ...
Fossil fuels are running out.	They are not renewable.	Why can't we make fossil fuels?
Burning fossil fuels causes global warming.	Burning fossil fuels makes the greenhouse gases increase.	What happens when global warming occurs? Why is it a problem?
We take fossil fuels for granted.	They are supplied to us everywhere — at the gas station and through electricity.	Why don't we find other types of fuel?

From *Energy of the Future* by Mandy Hager, Skyrider* Double Takes

Identifying cause-and-effect relationships

One way of analyzing a text is to look for relationships between events or actions. This can be done with fictional and informational texts. The students can use a graphic organizer to record the cause-and-effect relationships they notice. When they share their findings with a partner or group, ask them to identify any words or phrases the author has used to indicate the nature of the relationship.

Comparing versions

Students can compare two or more versions of a story, or two texts on the same topic, to identify the elements that are the same or different.

Tell them to make notes of details they want to remember so they can discuss them later. Some obvious examples would be the versions of fairy tales, pourquoi tales, and myths or legends that explain natural phenomena. If students are familiar with these versions, they can discuss the effects of the differences and how they might change the overall message of the story.

Chart information as you read – **analysis**
Connect this list of ideas:
What did you notice?
Were there differences? Did the differences matter? } **synthesis**
Discuss how the texts compare.

Identifying assumptions, points of view, and bias

This activity can be used with persuasive (argument) texts as well as reports, explanations, and narratives. Ask the students to:

- identify assumptions within a text (for example, that all logging is wrong, that girls are more interested in appearances than boys, or that everyone has a computer at home)
- analyze the development and sequence of ideas (for example, When and how did the author first introduce this idea? How did it develop?)
- analyze the information and the conclusions
- draw together (synthesize) the results of their analysis to form a conclusion.

The students can use headings to record ideas as they read.

The author said that ...
I think that ...

Or:

What I read	What I am thinking	What I learned

Comparing characters

This activity will be familiar to most students, but it can be developed to encourage a deeper analysis of characters and to synthesize ideas, for example, about the stereotypes in some kinds of literature. Students can use Venn diagrams or matrix charts to illustrate relationships between texts and between characters.

Using a story map

Students can use a story map to show how the elements of a narrative come together to create overall meaning. This strategy is used in tandem with that of identifying the main idea. As a partner activity, students can use their story map to retell a story and synthesize the reading.

Analyzing key messages

Use rich texts that have enough substance to generate good discussion of the key messages. Students can:

- record an idea they have learned from their reading and list facts about this idea
- analyze the parts of the text that have the key messages – the introduction, the body, the conclusion
- explain the key messages
- identify the evidence the author used to convey these messages
- identify evidence to support (or contradict) a point of view
- explain the relationship between two pieces of information
- explain how what they have read relates to what they already know
- explain how they can combine their new learning with their prior knowledge of a topic or idea.

Many of these activities draw on other comprehension strategies: point this out to the students as you encourage them to think metacognitively about what they do as they read and analyze a text.

Evaluating

Students make judgments based on their understanding of the text and their knowledge and values. They learn to evaluate whether what they have read is relevant. They also learn to evaluate based on the author's purpose and the author's position on particular issues. As they learn to evaluate text, students learn that not everything they read is factual or true and that authors bring their own personal experiences and perspectives to their writing.

Students learning to evaluate texts will:

- draw on their prior knowledge to ask and answer questions that will help them think about what they have read
- analyze and synthesize ideas
- recognize inconsistencies within messages or information
- recognize when an author is trying to influence their thinking with a particular point of view
- respond to the text in a personal yet informed way
- make judgments about what an author is saying
- describe and demonstrate to others how they arrived at their opinions.

Allow the students to practice this strategy in small groups, using the think-aloud approach to explain what opinions or evaluations they are forming and what strategies they are using to help them.

Possible learning goals

We are learning to:

- express opinions about a text as we evaluate it
- challenge the ideas presented by the author
- look for author bias within a text (a preconceived idea, an example of favoritism or prejudice)
- decide how effectively the text developed in view of the author's purpose and the intended audience
- decide if the text is relevant to our discussion, exploration, or research.

Supporting activities

Write learning goals that match the students' needs, then select one or more activities to share with the students. Explain the activity, adjusting the support to enable the students to eventually work on it independently. Many of the examples below can be adjusted to allow for different degrees of support, for example, by assigning the "What do you think?" tasks.

What do you think?

Students read or listen to a text. They then begin the process of learning to evaluate by selecting one or more of the following tasks. These can be written onto individual cards for random distribution and used in pairs or small groups for discussion. Examples are given but the range of responses will be much wider than these.

- Express an opinion (I think that …)
- Ask an evaluating question (Why do you think that …?)
- Challenge the text or the author (I don't believe … is right. In my opinion …)
- Look for bias (The author seems to be expressing a personal opinion rather than facts. I think this because …)
- Say how effectively the text was developed in view of the purpose and the audience (The author intended to … but in my opinion, he didn't convince me because …)

Challenge and justify

In this activity, students work in groups to challenge one another's evaluations of a text. Select texts that will stimulate discussion. These can be of almost any text type – even a shopping list could provoke discussion! The students can challenge or justify:

- the inclusion of a particular aspect or piece of information
- their own or their partner's evaluation of the text
- a recommendation of the text for other audiences
- an opinion on the content of the text, for example, the effectiveness of the author's style
- priorities within the text, for example, from most important to least important information; most interesting to least interesting character
- the overall effectiveness of the text
- whether the author met the purpose for which the text was written.

After discussing one of these challenges, the students can reflect on how the activity has helped them to evaluate the text.

When students struggle

When students struggle with comprehension, their problems may be linked to poor decoding skills and poor fluency, but this is not always the case. For many students, helping them focus on how to be a better comprehender is equally important. Other students, despite being good decoders, may struggle to comprehend and learn from text. Some readers may be confused about the purpose and use of comprehension strategies while other students may not have the strategies or the background knowledge to support their learning. For these students, comprehension instruction needs to be very explicit and structured to provide long term, step-by-step support.

Through carefully planned and monitored metacognitive comprehension instruction, teachers can make the necessary skills and strategies accessible and explicit, and they can support this with daily opportunities for guided, paired, and independent practice. When students receive intermittent or irregular instruction, or instruction that is not targeted at their specific needs, they are less likely to retain new learning from one lesson to the next. Regular, planned instruction that is based on the principles described in chapter 1 is critical for this group.

Students who struggle to comprehend text often do not have the metacognitive awareness that tells them when they are not understanding and what to do. Developing a highly metacognitive approach to teaching and learning with these students is essential in assisting them to become strategic readers.

This section should be read in conjunction with chapter 1 and with the earlier parts of this chapter that explain the comprehension strategies that students need to become effective readers. The critical factor is ensuring that the teacher has accurately identified each student's particular mix of instructional learning needs (which will likely also include decoding, vocabulary, and fluency needs) and has the knowledge to draw these together through targeted instruction.

It is important to keep groups small for instruction – a maximum of six to eight students should ensure that there are many of opportunities for active participation and that the teacher is able to observe and monitor each student's progress and difficulties. See chapters 6 and 7 for information about approaches and grouping arrangements.

While there are many approaches to working with students who struggle to comprehend written texts, this section examines some components of comprehension instruction that are particularly important:

- Making specific links to the student's prior knowledge
- Teaching students to monitor their comprehension
- Focusing on quality questioning and discussion
- Teaching students how to ask questions of the text
- Increasing the time spent reading high-quality texts.

Making specific connections to the student's prior knowledge

Making connections to prior knowledge involves building bridges between the student and the text. This includes making connections to the student's previous life experiences, making connections to a student's knowledge of the content of the text, and making connections to the student's knowledge of the structure of the text. Teachers need to know their students well and to use this knowledge to provide materials that connect to the lives of the students. Often, involving students in selecting a text is useful for making connections between a text and students' prior knowledge.

For students who struggle, it is important that teachers plan to develop and build connections to prior knowledge before, during, and after reading. This may involve spending extra time to prepare students for reading, for example, beginning with a mini-lesson to preteach a concept. The mini-lesson can be connected (through the learning goals) to content and skills from previous lessons. As reading progresses, the teacher checks on the links students are making between their prior knowledge and new information, and these can be discussed after the reading to reinforce the ways that making links can aid comprehension.

For every lesson and activity, teachers can give support by being specific about the learning goals and by spending time helping the students to reflect on and assess their learning throughout the lesson. Students can participate in discussions about their learning and can help the teacher to set the learning goal for the next day's session. As a final prompt, students can finish the lesson with a log entry to record what they have learned and what they need to focus on next.

In addition to the activities suggested earlier in this chapter, three further ways of linking to student prior knowledge are described below.

1. Making connections to prior knowledge through analogy

The teacher will share an analogy that connects the content of the new text to experiences that the students can relate to. Analogies are useful for helping students remember what they are reading, particularly when it is new to them. For example, if the text includes a discussion of famine, the teacher could develop an analogy.

> *It's a little like this: you wake up in the morning, and you are really hungry. You go to the kitchen and there is nothing for breakfast … and then there is nothing for lunch … and then there is nothing for dinner … and this happens day after day after day … no food in the house, no food at the supermarket, nothing to eat …*

2. Linking to prior knowledge through previewing

The teacher writes a preview of the text and presents it to the students before reading. Usually the preview includes a statement that will generate interest in the text, a brief overview of what the text is about, and one or two questions, statements, or opinions that will surface during reading. These questions are in addition to questions that are used to guide each section of text – see information about guided, shared, and reciprocal reading in chapter 6.

Preview
Overview
Questions to consider

We're going to be reading Joshua's Song *by Joan Hiatt Harlow.*

Preview

How would you feel if you had to leave school and work to support your family? What work would you be able to do if you were only thirteen?

Overview

The year is 1913, and a flu epidemic sweeping through America has killed Joshua's father. The family is suddenly poor, and Joshua is the only one who can go out to work. He finds a job selling newspapers, but the life is hard, and Joshua doesn't fit in well with the other sellers. His dream of joining the Boston Boys' Choir has faded, but when the city is threatened with a major disaster, Joshua finds he can help – in more ways than one.

Questions to consider

> *Do you think that hard times bring out the best in people?*

> *Is there a hero inside all of us? Can you imagine a situation in which you could be a hero?*

3. Making connections to prior knowledge by using textual and visual supports in the text

This approach involves walking students through the text prior to reading it, in the same way that primary teachers do with emergent level readers. The teacher works through the text, not reading the words but noticing and discussing the textual and visual supports. These include headings and subheadings, illustrations, diagrams, maps, charts, and tables. While this may take a little time, it should be viewed as valuable instruction time because it provides a strong base on which students can build their learning. It also gives the students a strategy that they can use when they encounter a difficult text.

Teaching students to monitor their comprehension

Students who struggle to comprehend rarely self-monitor and do not call on strategies to help them overcome difficulties. Self-monitoring is a practice that needs to be regularly and routinely reinforced. Students will benefit from deliberate instruction on how to monitor and how to recognize when they are not understanding their reading. This can be done through regular demonstrations where teachers and students show and explain what they are doing and why. It can also be done through the students "fix-up" strategies that they can use independently. Strategies that assist students to fix up faulty comprehension include:

- making notes of difficult words and ideas for discussion, using index cards or sticky notes
- summarizing the main points in the text, paragraph by paragraph (see example below)
- identifying parts of text that are problematic and need clarifying, using sticky notes
- using supports such as cue cards for visualization (see example below)
- using supports to make inferences (see example below).

Teachers can provide supports such as graphic organizers that students can add to as they read. Graphic organizers are also useful in helping students to self-monitor and take control of their comprehension, but they should never be used as worksheets that students are left to complete without purpose or discussion. *Some further examples of graphic organizers are discussed in chapter 7 from page 263.*

Summarizing

Using a template, teachers and students can identify the important ideas in a text and record them, section by section. The teacher models writing a summary statement and supports the students to write one summary for each of the important ideas.

Page or Chapter	Important Ideas	Summary Statement

Making inferences

The teacher models using a graphic organizer and works through one or two examples with the students before they use it independently or in pairs.

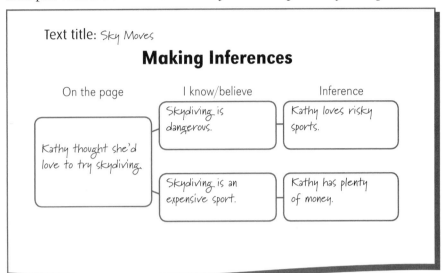

From *Sky Moves* by Pat Quinn, Skyrider* Shared Reading nonfiction

Visualizing

A graphic organizer is used as a prompt for students to identify the important details in descriptive or explanatory texts.

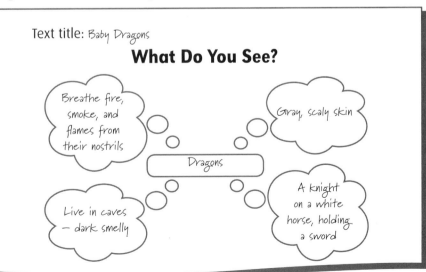

From *Baby Dragons* by Rod Morris, Skyrider* Shared Reading nonfiction

Focusing on quality questioning and discussion

For all students, the quality and nature of questioning and discussion is critical to determining what students are retaining and understanding. Questioning led by the teacher needs to discover:

- what the students understand
- where misunderstandings are occurring
- what students are doing when they do not understand
- how well students are able to explain their own processing of text
- how students are progressing toward the learning goals of the lesson
- what students know about their understanding of the text.

It is equally important for teachers to move interactions away from straight question-and-answer routines and toward discussion around the text and the strategies. As teachers focus on the effectiveness of their questions and the discussions that they generate, they need to avoid situations where:

- not enough "wait time" is allowed (increasing the pause from one to three seconds makes a marked difference to the quality of responses)
- questions are not clear, leading to confusion
- questions are asked in quick succession without giving students time to respond to the first
- teachers answers their own questions
- the teacher's responses are evaluative ("Good," "Right!" "Yes") without providing support for students to take the next steps to build their understanding.

Teaching students how to ask questions of the text

This comprehension strategy is discussed in depth earlier in this chapter. When students are struggling to comprehend, asking questions of the text is difficult. If they do not monitor or understand fully what they are reading, they are not able to ask questions. The following activity can be used in a variety of ways to support student questioning of texts.

Questioning the text

Divide the text into small sections and involve all students in asking questions at the end of each section. You may need to include prompts to help students to phrase their questions and to encourage them to ask a variety of questions. Examples of prompts include:

- What, why, how, who, where, when
- If … , then …
- Do you know … ?
- I wonder …
- How could this happen?
- What would be a reason for this?
- What impact or result will this have?
- Why did the character think this?
- Why has the author told us this?

Increasing the time spent reading high-quality texts

For all students who struggle, a great deal of time spent reading high-quality texts is essential. The match to reading level is very important: gains will only be made when the texts are at the students' independent reading level. In addition to instructional lessons and daily partner reading (see also chapters 6 and 7), being read to by an adult several times a day provides increased opportunities for exposure to a variety of quality texts. This could include high-quality picture books written for older students (for example, the wordless picture books by Jeannie Baker, Anno Mitsumasa, and David Wiesner), as well as different kinds of factual texts and novels. Through these, students can encounter new ideas, confront different points of view, see a narrative progressing, and develop empathy with characters, events, settings, and plots. The more exposure to texts the better!

Extending able readers

Students who are able to comprehend a variety of texts will be able to integrate comprehension strategies according to the kind of text they are reading. These students will be able to explain what they are doing as they comprehend and what they do when they realize that they do not comprehend. Effective programs for this group of learners will also seek to promote active and challenging engagement with text. There are a number of ways that this can be achieved. This section explores five of these. They are:

- Supporting strategy use with increasingly complex texts
- Student-generated previewing of texts
- Student development of graphic organizers
- Challenging students with diverse reading
- Focusing on connections.

Supporting strategy use with increasingly complex texts

As this group of students read widely and encounter increasingly complex texts, teaching needs to extend their self-monitoring strategies. Students may not be able to articulate the strategies they use to comprehend difficult texts. Instruction tailored to the needs of these students will include:

- identifying the kinds of text they find most difficult – this can be done by asking students themselves and by monitoring their comprehension
- providing direct instruction on strategies that will support their comprehension
- ensuring that this instruction can be applied across the curriculum
- giving students responsibility for instructional reading by choosing texts themselves and holding discussions using a literature circle approach (see chapter 6)
- involving students in setting their learning goals and success criteria, in self-assessing, in monitoring, and in discussing their learning regularly with their teachers and their peers.

Student-generated previewing of texts

Students can work in pairs to provide a preview for the instructional lesson. The teacher will initially provide instruction on how to preview (see page 184). However, as students take more responsibility, they can develop their own preview specific to the text type and their purpose for reading the text. For example, a group is reading historical fiction with a view to understanding life in the seventeenth century. The preview contained key vocabulary, events, and ideas to support connections that the students could make to information they previously learned.

Student development of graphic organizers

Students can be shown how to design their own graphic organizers appropriate to the purpose of their reading. This allows the students to extend responsibility in their learning as they work with the teacher to identify the kind of graphic organizer that will be appropriate for the lesson and for retrieving or organizing the required information.

The graphic organizers should reflect the learning goals and be used by the students to interpret text. As students explore relationships among texts, they can develop a range of graphic organizers to record their learning.

Graphic organizers can also be developed for students to explore the literal and figurative meanings of words and to show relationships between characters and settings, between texts written by the same author, and between content covering the same topic.

Challenging students with diverse reading

Able readers need many opportunities to read widely. As part of this program, developing a book club for students is useful in encouraging them to read texts that they might not normally select. A book club is based on regular meetings: participants meet (perhaps every two weeks) to discuss a text that they have read. They share excerpts from the text, discuss the content and style, and evaluate and share their responses. Often the texts are selected based on an author study (students may each read a different text by the same author) or theme (students each read a different text on a similar theme). Texts can be interchanged among the group. Several established teaching approaches such as questioning the author (Beck, et. al., 1997), author's chair (Graves, 1994), and literature circles (Daniels, 1994; Roser and Martinez, 1995) can be incorporated into a book club approach as a way of challenging students towards wider and more diverse reading.

See chapter 7 for more information on these approaches.

Focusing on connections

Able readers can be encouraged to look for connections across texts and within a text – sentence to sentence connections, paragraph to paragraph connections, paragraph to illustration connections. If students are exposed to a variety of texts, including sophisticated picture books, they can explore examples of points of view, irony, symbolism, and setting and discuss how these have been developed. From focusing on connections, students can see how major ideas, topics, and themes can relate not only to their reading but also to their writing.

Developing metacognitive awareness

All of the activities described above encourage students to develop a metacognitive awareness of the strategies that they can use to increase their reading comprehension. By modeling the use of comprehension strategies and by using metacognitive comprehension instruction (see chapter 1), teachers can develop students' awareness of what they are learning about how they comprehend texts. This happens most readily through high-quality dialogue between the teacher and the students and between students.

When students take over the responsibility for monitoring their comprehension (see page 185), they are able to develop metacognitive awareness of their own understanding, and they can provide support in the form of feedback and advice to one another.

Summary

Comprehension improves when teachers design and implement activities that support students' understanding of texts. Such instruction needs to occur regularly and is best conducted with small groups.

This chapter has focused on deliberately teaching students to use a variety of comprehension strategies. These strategies may be used prior to reading, during reading, and at the conclusion of reading. On all occasions, teachers are encouraged to ensure that their students are actively involved in talking about the strategies they are drawing on, explaining how they used a specific strategy as they read a section of text, modeling for others their use of the strategy, questioning others on their strategy use, using the think-aloud approach, asking for feedback on their strategy use, and providing peer feedback on strategy use.

Comprehension instruction increases teachers' awareness of the importance of the prompts and questions to assist students to internalize strategies. Examples of prompts and questions include:

- What strategies are you choosing to use here?
- How are you using them?
- When there is a difficult section of text, you may choose to use the … strategy.
- I suggest you …
- Have you thought of …?
- Have you tried …?
- What strategy do you think will help you in this part of the text?
- How will you know if you are understanding as you read this part of the text?
- Look ahead to see what might help you with this next section.
- How are you going toward achieving your reading goal? How do you know?

It is important to remember that the aim is the independent, flexible, and coordinated use of comprehension strategies. The degree of support required by individual students will vary. Not all students will need to be taught all of these strategies. Some will need extended practice with one. Teachers provide this through metacognitive comprehension instruction based on the identified needs of their students and the feedback they receive. The ultimate goal must be for the students to use the strategies unassisted and automatically.

References and recommended reading

Anderson, R. C. and Pearson, P. D. (1984). "A Schema-theoretic View of Basic Processes in Reading". In *Handbook of Reading Research*, ed. P. D. Pearson. New York, New York: Longman, pp. 255–291.

Beck, I. L., McKeown, M. G., Hamilton, R. L., and Kucan, L. (1997). *Questioning the Author: An Approach for Enhancing Student Engagement with Text.* Newark, Delaware: International Reading Association.

Block, C. C. and Pressley, M. (2001). *Comprehension Instruction: Research-based Best Practices.* New York, New York: The Guilford Press.

Daniels, H. (1994). *Literature Circles: Voice and Choice in the Student-Centered Classroom.* York, Maine: Stenhouse.

Dowhower, S. L. (1999). "Supporting a Strategic Stance in the Classroom: A Comprehension Framework for Helping Teachers Help Students to be Strategic". *The Reading Teacher*, 52(7), pp. 672–683.

Duffy, G. G. (2003). *Explaining Reading: A Resource for Teaching Concepts, Skills, and Strategies.* New York, New York: The Guilford Press.

Duke, N. K. and Pearson, P. D. (2002). "Effective Practices for Developing Reading Comprehension". In *What Research Has to Say about Reading Instruction*, ed. A. E. Farstrup and S. J. Samuels (3rd ed.). Newark, Delaware: International Reading Association, pp. 205–242.

Expert Panel on Literacy in Grades 4 to 6 in Ontario (2004). *Literacy for Learning: The Report of the Expert Panel on Literacy in Grades 4 to 6 in Ontario.* Ontario Ministry of Education.

Farstrup. A. E. and Samuels, S. J. ed. (2002) *What Research Has to Say About Reading Instruction.* (3rd ed.). Newark, Delaware: International Reading Association.

Fountas, I. and Pinnell, G. S. (2001). *Guiding Readers and Writers (Grades 3–6): Teaching Comprehension, Genre, and Content Literacy.* Portsmouth, New Hampshire: Heinemann.

Graves, D. (1994). *A Fresh Look at Writing.* Portsmouth, New Hampshire: Heinemann.

Keene, E. O., and Zimmerman, S. (1997). *Mosaic of Thought: Teaching Comprehension in a Reader's Workshop.* Portsmouth, New Hampshire: Heinemann.

Marzano, R. J., Pickering, D. J., and Pollock, J. E. (2001). *Classroom Instruction That Works: Research-based Strategies for Improving Student Achievement.* Alexandria, Virginia: Association for Supervision and Curriculum Development.

Ministry of Education (2004). *Effective Literacy Practice in Years 1 to 4.* Wellington, New Zealand: Learning Media.

Ministry of Education (2006). *Effective Literacy Practice in Years 5 to 8.* Wellington, New Zealand: Learning Media.

Ogle, D. (1986). "K-W-L: A Teaching Model That Develops Action Reading of Expository Text". *The Reading Teacher*, 39. pp. 564–570.

Pressley, M. (1998). *Reading Instruction That Works: The Case for Balanced Teaching.* New York, New York: The Guilford Press.

Pressley, M. (2001, September). "Comprehension Instruction: What Makes Sense Now, What Might Make Sense Soon". *Reading Online*, 5(2). www.readingonline.org/articles/art_index. asp?HREF = articles/handbook/pressley/index. html

Pressley, M. (2002). *Reading Instruction That Works: The Case for Balanced Teaching.* (2nd ed.). New York, New York: The Guilford Press.

Pressley, M. (2006). *Reading Instruction That Works: The Case for Balanced Teaching.* (3rd ed.). New York, New York: The Guilford Press.

Pressley, M., Allington, R. L., Wharton-McDonald, R., Collins-Block, C., and Morrow, L. (2001). *Learning to Read: Lessons from Exemplary First Grade Classrooms.* New York, New York: The Guilford Press.

Pressley M. and El-Dinary, P. B. (1997). "What We Know about Translating Comprehension Strategies Instruction Research into Practice". *Journal of Learning Disabilities*, 30, pp. 486–488.

Raphael, T. and Au, K. H. (2005). "Q. A. R.: Enhancing Comprehension and Test Taking Across Grades and Content Areas". *The Reading Teacher*, 59(3), pp. 206–221.

Roser, N. and Martinez, M. ed. (1995). *Book Talk and Beyond: Children and Teachers Respond to Literature.* Newark, Delaware: International Reading Association.

Stead, T. (2005). *Reality Checks: Teaching Reading Comprehension with Nonfiction K-5.* Markham, Ontario: Pembroke Publishers Ltd; Portland, Maine: Stenhouse.

Trabasso,T. and Bouchard, E. (2002.) "Teaching Readers How to Comprehend Text Strategically". In *Comprehension Instruction: Research-Based Best Practices*, ed. C. Block and M. Pressley, New York, New York: The Guilford Press, pp. 176–200.

Williams, J. P. (2002). "Reading Comprehension Strategies and Teacher Preparation". In *What Research Has to Say about Reading Instruction*, ed. A. E. Farstrup and S. J. Samuels, (3rd ed.). Newark, Delaware: International Reading Association, pp. 243–260.

APPENDIX 5.1

Oral student survey 1

What do you do in your head to help you understand what you read?

- · Connect what I'm reading to things I already know
- · Guess what's going to come next
- · Make a picture in my mind
- · Read between the lines
- · Ask myself questions
- · Go back and reread
- · Summarize as I'm reading
- · Look for the big idea or message
- · Use other ways to understand, for example, by recalling the sequence of events or the relationships between characters in a story

Now circle the ones you would like to learn more about to help you understand what you read.

APPENDIX 5.2

Oral student survey 2

Here's a list of some of the comprehension strategies that you can use to help you understand what you read. Circle those that you would like to learn more about.

- Connect what I'm reading to things I already know (making connections)
- Guess what's going to come next (predicting)
- Make a picture in my mind (visualizing)
- Read between the lines (inferring)
- Ask myself questions (self-questioning)
- Go back and reread (seeking clarification)
- Summarize as I'm reading (summarizing)
- Look for the big idea or message (identifying main idea)
- Use other ways to understand, for example, by recalling the sequence of events or the relationships between characters (analyzing and synthesizing)

Oral student survey 3

Here's a list of some of the comprehension strategies that readers use to help them understand what they read.

- · Connect what I'm reading to things I already know (making connections)
- · Guess what's going to come next (predicting)
- · Make a picture in my mind (visualizing)
- · Read between the lines (inferring)
- · Ask myself questions (self-questioning)
- · Go back and reread (seeking clarification)
- · Summarize as I'm reading (summarizing)
- · Look for the big idea or message (identifying main idea)
- · Use other ways to understand, for example, by recalling the sequence of events or the relationships between characters (analyzing and synthesizing)

Describe how you use some or all of the strategies on this list. For each strategy you use, tell me:

What the strategy does to help you _____

How you use the strategy _____

When you use the strategy _____

Please list any other strategies that you use and describe how you use them.

Which comprehension strategies are most useful to you as you read? Circle them on the list.

Instructional Reading Approaches

This chapter begins by discussing three instructional approaches to teaching reading comprehension that are highly metacognitive and that support students to become active participants in their own reading. These approaches are shared reading, guided reading, and reciprocal reading. Each approach uses group-based instruction. The chapter covers four additional approaches that can be used to support shared, guided, or reciprocal reading. These are questioning the author, literature circles, repeated paired reading, and readers' theater.

Key messages for teachers

- Effective teachers use a variety of instructional approaches to provide reading comprehension instruction in decoding, word recognition, fluency, accuracy, vocabulary, and comprehension strategies.
- These approaches are highly metacognitive.
- A balance of teaching approaches is necessary when planning.
- Approaches should be selected based on the purpose of the lesson, the amount of support and direct instruction the students require, the degree of explicit teaching versus independent practice required, and the organization of the class.

Metacognitive Reading Approaches			
Key approaches:	**Shared Reading**	**Guided Reading**	**Reciprocal Reading**
Supported by:			
Questioning the author	Literature circles	Repeated paired reading	Readers' theater

Each approach provides opportunities for students to discuss, demonstrate, explain, share, and question both the content of their reading and their use of comprehension strategies. They provide for small-group interaction and enable active participation in the process of gaining meaning from text and learning about learning. Formative assessment and transactional strategy instruction are an integral component of each of these approaches (see also chapter 1).

Reading aloud

As well as the instructional approaches described in this chapter, the practice of reading aloud to students remains a powerful and important approach through all grade levels. When teachers select and read texts that will engage their students, they are able to demonstrate their own enjoyment of reading, the thinking and thoughtfulness that mature readers use, and the technical skills (such as fluency) of an expert reader. Reading aloud also contributes to a sense community in the classroom: this in turn can support the development of a metacognitive approach to reading comprehension as students share their understandings with one another.

Using questions

As discussed briefly in chapter 5, rich questions are an essential tool in metacognitive comprehension instruction. All of the approaches discussed in this chapter use questions as a way of starting and continuing discussions about texts. The questions that are most likely to create deeper learning are carefully planned and probe beneath the surface of understanding. These "rich" questions require students to make an inference, to offer a reflection, to give and justify an opinion, or to ask their own questions. By using rich questioning, teachers model the kinds of questions they want students to ask. These are some examples of rich questions:

- Why do you think that? What clues support your answer?
- What does the author want you to think? What words indicate this?
- Can you explain why or how this happened?
- What other opinions might people hold about this? Could any of these be justified?
- How does the layout of the text help you to make sense of this topic?
- What did you notice about …?

- If you were able to change the outcome, what would you do and why?
- Where could you find out more about this issue?
- How do you know that the facts are correct? Why might a writer use some facts and not others?

Shared reading

What is shared reading?

Shared reading (Allen, 2002; Brown, 2004; Expert Panel on Literacy, 2004; Holdaway, 1979) is an important approach for teaching reading comprehension, particularly for approaching material in textbooks. Shared reading is often used for large-group and whole-class lessons, but it is also a strong approach for group instruction in reading. It allows teachers and students to focus on learning a variety of reading strategies, including word recognition, vocabulary, fluency, and comprehension strategies.

In shared reading, all students can see a large copy of the text (for example, a poster, a big book, a chart, an overhead projector, or a CD-ROM projected onto a screen or whiteboard) or they may each have a copy of the text. The teacher takes responsibility for most of the reading.

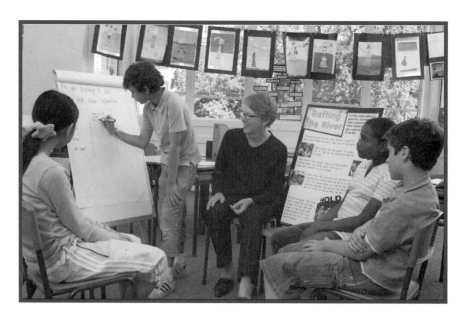

As the teacher reads the text aloud, the students participate through active listening and through their engagement in discussions that focus on the use of strategies for word recognition, vocabulary, and comprehension. They attend to modeling and explanations from the teacher and engage in collaborative problem solving based on the challenges within the text. This can include the students modeling, explaining, and asking questions too: their engagement in learning is active.

Because the teacher takes responsibility for most of the reading, shared reading allows students to have access to texts that are at a higher level than they would be able to read independently. This means that shared reading can support students to read texts that would otherwise be too difficult for them as well as model reading in a new or unfamiliar genre. As the teacher reads aloud, the students follow along silently or join in when asked.

The teacher identifies the reading comprehension needs of the students and sets appropriate learning goals. The teacher then selects a text that will match the learning goals and the students' experiences and interests (for example, a text that supports a current science or social studies topic). The teacher also considers the degree of support and challenge that the text will offer and how to best support the students through the lesson.

Shared reading provides opportunities for:
- explicit modeling of fluent reading by the teacher (see chapter 4)
- explicit demonstration of the thinking that occurs when making meaning (see chapter 5)
- teacher modeling and discussion of comprehension strategies (see chapter 5), word recognition strategies (see chapter 2), and vocabulary strategies (see chapter 3)
- practice and internalization of strategies to develop metacognition (see chapter 1)
- the teacher and the students to engage in discussion to figure out the meaning of text together.

Steps in a shared reading lesson

Planning the lesson

Planning starts with the teacher analyzing assessment data and determining a clear learning goal. The teacher selects a text that will match the purpose and that will provide suitable opportunities for instruction. During a careful reading of the text prior to the lesson, the teacher will identify any potential challenges and determine how to develop the key teaching points. Key questions can be noted on the lesson plan for easy access during the lesson. Depending on the purpose, the teacher may want to cover some parts of the text (for example, masking a vocabulary word that the students will need to figure out from the context or covering a paragraph to encourage predictions).

Introducing the text

The learning goal is shared in writing with the students. The teacher explains this, discusses it with the students, and checks that they are clear on the main purpose of the lesson. The teacher and the students develop the success criteria, through which they can determine whether the lesson goal has been met. Discussion will enable all students to be clear on the main goal. The teacher will also plan to link the theme, key idea, or topic to the students' prior knowledge to prepare them for the reading. Based on this, the students may share their expectations of the text (for suggestions about making connections with prior knowledge, refer to chapter 5 and chapter 7).

Reading and discussing the text

Unless the text is particularly short or it requires a complete read through, the teacher can divide the text into sections for reading. The teacher shares the purpose for each section, then reads them aloud while the students follow silently or join in. Between each section, the teacher demonstrates strategies used to make meaning and uses the think-aloud approach to make these strategies explicit. The teacher then involves the students in modeling and explaining to their peers how they made meaning from the text.

Through careful questioning and discussion, the teacher makes links to the learning goal and ensures that all students understand the key ideas and messages during reading. This may include examining the structures and techniques used by the author and looking at the author's purpose. The students are encouraged to ask questions of the text and of one another as they develop their understanding and their use of the focus strategies.

The lesson continues with sections of text being read aloud while the students are encouraged to be active participants in thinking, discussing, demonstrating, questioning, and modeling.

Lesson conclusion

At the conclusion of the lesson, the teacher revisits the key ideas and areas of learning (based on the learning goals). Discussion centers on what was comprehended and the strategies the students have used. The students self-assess their learning (using the success criteria) and, with the teacher, set their next learning goals.

A follow-up task may be set for students to complete either as a group, in pairs, or on their own. This task should be designed to build on the learning in the lesson.

The Shared Reading Procedure

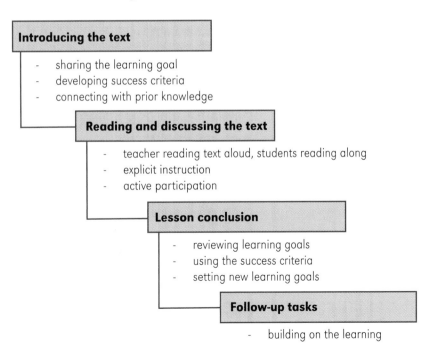

Introducing the text
- sharing the learning goal
- developing success criteria
- connecting with prior knowledge

Reading and discussing the text
- teacher reading text aloud, students reading along
- explicit instruction
- active participation

Lesson conclusion
- reviewing learning goals
- using the success criteria
- setting new learning goals

Follow-up tasks
- building on the learning

Using the shared reading approach to support learning

In this section, we go "inside" the shared reading lesson to see how metacognitive instruction can be achieved.

Inside the shared reading lesson

Planning the lesson

The teacher gathers data to determine the students' needs.

A group of students in Mr. Weisswasser's class is having difficulty visualizing as they read, and they tend to skip over unknown vocabulary. His analysis will affect:

a. text selection – the teaching will focus on texts or excerpts that have rich language to help the students form visual images as they read. The texts will also contain some unfamiliar vocabulary that could be approached by using context clues;

b. the questions he will ask and the text and language features he will draw attention to during each reading of the text;

c. the type of follow-up activities he will set at the end of the lesson and to prepare for subsequent lessons that focus on visualization and finding the meanings of new vocabulary.

The teacher may use a series of mini-lessons to introduce the focus comprehension strategy to the students by explaining the strategy and when and why to use it and by illustrating this with a variety of texts.

The strategy of visualizing is important because it:

> *deepens our understanding of the text*
> *helps us to remember what we've read*
> *helps us relate to the text personally.*

We use this strategy by thinking about:

> *what we "see" as we read: imagining the people, actions, settings, or events*
> *the words and phrases the author has used to help us "see" this*
> *how the pictures in our minds build and grow as we read through the text.*

When the students are beginning to understand the strategy, the teacher moves the strategy instruction into the shared reading lesson. The teacher selects an appropriate text for instruction, identifying any potential challenges that the students may encounter.

Mr. Weisswasser explains his choice:

I've chosen a text that uses rich descriptive language and will provide good opportunities for visualization and for figuring out new vocabulary. I have recorded any particular text features or challenging language on sticky notes for reference during the lesson. I plan how to introduce these prior to reading.

Introducing the text

The teacher introduces the text by making deliberate links between the content, the overall theme, the text structure, and the students' prior knowledge. This is to ensure that the students are prepared for reading in terms of both the content and the structure.

> *This is a text about a family who crash their travel craft. They don't know where they are or if they will ever be rescued. They try to build a fire and make a shelter to keep them safe while they wait to be rescued. Without food, water, and warmth, waiting to be rescued is hard work, and the family face a number of challenges.*

The learning goal and success criteria are shared with the students. The teacher reminds the students of what they have already learned about the focus comprehension strategy.

> *We are learning to get a "picture in our minds" as we read by:*
> > *listening to the details that the author has used*
> > *using our prior knowledge of the words and of what the author is describing*
> > *using this strategy to develop a better understanding of the text.*
>
> *We will be successful when we can:*
> > *identify the words the author has used to describe the impact of the crash and the actions of the characters*
> > *think about our own experiences and use these links to form a picture of the family preparing a shelter*
> > *talk about the pictures we saw, and explain how visualizing has helped us to understand the text better.*

The teacher discusses any unusual text features and possible challenges with the students. This includes introducing important vocabulary that students may not know, or the teacher may remind the students of strategies that they have already learned – for example, figuring out words from the context.

Reading and discussing the text

The teacher sets a purpose for the text and reads it aloud, carefully modeling the behaviors of a fluent reader (see also chapter 4). While the teacher is reading aloud, the students follow along with their eyes or join in if they wish to.

The teacher then discusses what has been read and where and how the focus strategy can be used to comprehend the text. The teacher leads a discussion about what these words and phrases mean to the students and what they might mean in the context of the text.

The students demonstrate the words and phrases that are helping them to visualize. Mr. Weisswasser then invites them to share the words and phrases they think are effective in painting a picture in their minds. He lists them on the whiteboard for discussion. Students then question one another about what they "see" (or hear or feel) as they read and why.

Mr. Weisswasser highlights some key features and uses questions and thinking aloud to prompt discussion:

> *Hit with a sledgehammer – what does this make you think of? How would you feel? What image does this give you of how Darnek feels?*

> *Slumped – does this make you sense that Shula is OK? What do you "see" when you read the word slumped?*

> *Imagine what happened before the craft crashed. Let's read again what Darnek could remember.*
> *I can hear the noise coming from the panel – that would be scary and I think very loud ... the flashing emergency strobe – that seems to me as if it would be bright and flashing quite quickly – it would worry me to see that ...*

Other examples to discuss with students:

· cautiously pulling himself upright

· groggily.

from "Strangers in the Landscape" by Anna Mackenzie, *On the Edge*, Orbit* Collections

The teacher then sets a purpose for reading the second section of text and reads it aloud, again modeling fluent reading behaviors. The teacher may draw the students' attention to some of these behaviors (for example, when emphasizing an action or feeling).

Mr. Weisswasser asks questions to gauge the students' understanding of what has been read and to encourage dialogue around the important ideas. He will use the think-aloud approach to explain what they are visualizing and how the text supported this image. Students will be invited to share the image they are gaining and the clues in the text that helped them.

When I read this, I visualized ... These words and this phrase helped me because ...

The students were also invited to draw what they saw, and (for one or two students) to label their drawings using evidence from the text and their prior knowledge. Mr. Weisswasser's questions included:

> *What do you think the author is trying to show us?*
> *What helps you to think this?*
> *What do you have to do with this information to help you create meaning?*

The sequence of setting the purpose, teacher reading, discussion, strategy focus, think-aloud, and demonstration continues as the text proceeds, with the students contributing to the teaching and learning. Finally, the teacher reads the text through aloud to enable the students to hear it as a whole once more.

The teacher explains the follow-up task (if one has been set) and links it to the learning goals. The students complete this as a group, in pairs, or on their own.

Reflecting on practice

An observation guide to support reading comprehension instruction through shared reading is provided in appendix 6.1 (page 242). Teachers will find this useful as a reference for reflecting on their own shared reading practice or to refine a particular aspect of shared reading. The guide can also be used by teachers as part of their ongoing professional development. Teachers observing others and providing support and feedback is a powerful form of professional development. The observation guide and the criteria can be used to guide feedback and set future professional development goals.

Guided reading
What is guided reading?

Guided reading (Clay, 1991; Expert Panel on Literacy, 2004; Fountas and Pinnell, 2001; Mooney, 1988; Rog, 2003) is a small-group approach in which students with similar instructional needs are grouped together for explicit comprehension instruction. Students are supported as they read, think, talk, and question their way through a text.

The texts need to be selected carefully to ensure a good match with the students' instructional needs, their reading level (no more than five to ten unknown words in every hundred), and their interests and experiences. Teachers can also take into account current topic or content-area studies.

Reading levels

Reading levels of texts are determined by analyzing the challenges relative to the supports for a particular reader. Selecting texts for guided reading is based on the students' learning needs, and a text should generally have no more than five to ten difficulties in every one hundred words. Although many educational texts now use a variety of leveling systems, teachers will still need to compare the text with what they know about their students. Prior knowledge (of the content, the genre, the vocabulary, or the concepts) varies greatly and will make a difference to whether a book is at a suitable reading level.

Steps in a guided reading lesson
Planning the lesson

Planning starts with the analysis of data to identify the students' needs. From this initial analysis, teachers make decisions about suitable grouping (see chapter 7 for more information about grouping). Based on the assessment data about the group, the teacher then decides on the learning goals (see page 22) and selects a text that will be suitable for the lesson's purpose and to meet the students' needs.

The teacher will need to read the text carefully to identify the possible challenges and supports. The teacher makes decisions about how the challenges will be approached. This could include providing a definition of an unknown word or showing a picture to make a new concept clearer. The teacher will also plan how to use the supports to make connections between the students' prior knowledge and the new ideas in the text.

Introducing the text

A guided reading lesson will often start with the teacher making deliberate links between the text and the students' prior knowledge. This could include telling the students what kind of text they will be reading and what the text is about (for example, sharing the main idea, the topic, or the theme or giving a hint of what is to come). Where necessary, the teacher will tell, model, or explain a new concept to clarify it and prepare the students for reading. The learning goal for the lesson is shared with the students, and the teacher checks that they understand the main purpose of the lesson. Any challenges that the teacher has identified are clarified with the students. Sometimes this will be unfamiliar vocabulary, or it may have to do with the structure or the genre of the text.

Reading and discussing the text

A guided reading lesson usually follows a pattern where explicit instruction (that can include modeling, explaining, questioning, and discussion) alternates with independent reading of manageable sections or "chunks." The teacher assigns a section of text for the students to read, perhaps one or two paragraphs to start with, and sets a purpose for that reading. For example:

- I want you to read the first two paragraphs to find out ...
- When you read the first paragraph, you will be introduced to the two main characters. Read to find out who they are and how they are related to one another.
- As you read, start thinking about some predictions you could make about this book.

The students read the section independently. This is most often silent reading although students may vocalize quietly to themselves if needed. The teacher monitors the students as they read, looking for any sign of confusion or difficulty. When students have read the assigned section, the teacher develops their understanding of what they have read by using metacognitive instructional strategies such as:

Sectioning the text

The text is sectioned or chunked to ensure that adequate support can be given as the reading progresses. The amount of text in each section will depend on the amount of challenge it will present to the particular group. In some cases, a chunk may be a paragraph, or two or three paragraphs. For texts that present fewer challenges, whole pages or even short chapters may be assigned.

- questioning students about what they have read and asking them to provide evidence for their responses;
- encouraging students to ask questions and explain the reasons for their questions;
- deliberately relating what has been read to the students' prior knowledge;
- encouraging discussion about what the students knew previously and what they have learned from the text;
- encouraging discussion around the main ideas in the text so far. This discussion is led by both the teacher and the students – encouraging students to take a lead in discussion;
- creating opportunities for students, as well as the teacher, to demonstrate the use of strategies (which can include strategies for word recognition, vocabulary, or comprehension, or a combination of these) by modeling or explaining, using the think-aloud approach. Student demonstration and thinking aloud is a critical component of metacognitive comprehension instruction;
- encouraging the students to explain their thinking to others.

When the teacher is confident that the students have a good understanding of the section, a second section is assigned (the amount assigned will depend on the number of challenges presented). The teacher sets a purpose to focus the reading, and students read this section independently.

Once again, the teacher asks questions and generates discussion to ascertain the students' understanding of what they have read, the strategies that they used to assist them, and the purpose and key message the author wishes to portray. The teacher encourages the students to respond to the messages in the text and refers back to the learning goal to review how well the students are achieving this.

When the teacher is satisfied that students are developing a clear understanding of the text, a third section is assigned, a purpose given, and students commence reading. Thus the guided reading procedure continues as teachers and students read, talk, question, and problem solve their way through the text.

The Guided Reading Procedure

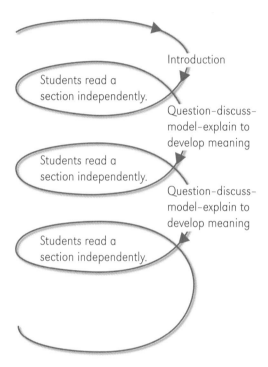

Introduction

Students read a section independently.

Question–discuss–model–explain to develop meaning

Students read a section independently.

Question–discuss–model–explain to develop meaning

Students read a section independently.

Lesson conclusion

When the reading is finished, the teacher and students discuss what they have read, what they did to comprehend the text, what they found difficult, and how they used strategies to solve problems. They reflect on the learning goal and determine how well they are achieving this. Together, they set goals for the next reading session. Teachers usually plan for and assign an independent follow-up activity so students will continue to develop their comprehension of the text before their next lesson. This activity is always related to the learning goal, the needs of the group, and the content of the text.

Guided reading is an approach to teaching reading comprehension that can be used with a variety of texts – both fiction and nonfiction, including chapter books, novels, short stories, magazine and journal articles, and even graphic texts. The key consideration is chunking the text into meaningful sections, followed by in-depth and student-centered discussion, questioning, and reflection of the key messages and purposes of the text. Where longer texts are used (for example, trade novels and chapter books) teachers often use guided reading to focus on selected chapters or excerpts (those sections that contain greater challenge, introduce new ideas, have complex plot structures, and so on) while other sections are assigned to be read independently by students.

Using the guided reading approach to support learning

In this section, we go "inside" the guided reading lesson to see how teachers make decisions about comprehension strategy instruction.

Inside the guided reading lesson

Planning the lesson

The teacher gathers data to determine the students' instructional needs and places the class into groups.

Mr. Rodriguez discusses his grade 4 class:

One group of students has difficulty inferring from narrative text. They don't regularly use context clues to assist them with unknown vocabulary and do not regard punctuation as they read. My analysis will affect:

> *text selection – my teaching will focus on a variety of narrative texts or excerpts that require students to infer information. These texts will be at a level appropriate to the reading abilities of the group;*

> *the questions I will ask and the text and language features that I will draw attention to during each reading of the text;*

> *the kind of follow-up activities that I will set at the conclusion of the lesson and in preparation for subsequent lessons on inference.*

The teacher provides a series of mini-lessons or a shared reading lesson to introduce the comprehension strategy to the students. The teacher explains the strategy with information about when and why it is useful and provides examples of it using extracts of text (see also chapter 5).

Mr. Rodriguez tells the group:
Inferring is an important strategy because it:
> *helps us to see meanings that are not stated directly in the text*
> *helps us to recognize and respond to clues the author gives us*
> *helps us to develop links between the information in the text and the key messages the author is conveying*
> *helps us to remember and reapply what we have read*
> *helps us to predict, interpret, form conclusions, and reason.*

> *We use this strategy by:*
> *going beyond the literal meaning to think about other meanings that might not be stated in the text*
> *making connections between our prior knowledge and the details, ideas, and concepts the author is telling us about and reaching our own conclusions based on these connections*
> *discussing, restating, and reflecting on the ideas in text.*

When the students are beginning to understand the strategy, the teacher moves the instruction into the guided reading lesson. The teacher determines the learning goal based on the students' needs and formative assessment techniques that may include discussion, structured observation, and anecdotal notes.

The primary goal for this series of lessons is to support the students as they learn how to infer. However, I also want to focus on teaching the students to use context clues to figure out the meaning of unknown words. In second and subsequent readings, I will have students practice this in pairs – discussing meanings of words as they read and giving one another feedback on their use of punctuation when they read for meaning.

The teacher selects a text that is suitable for the students' reading levels and that has scope for the planned instruction. The teacher reads the text and identifies any potential challenges that the students may encounter.

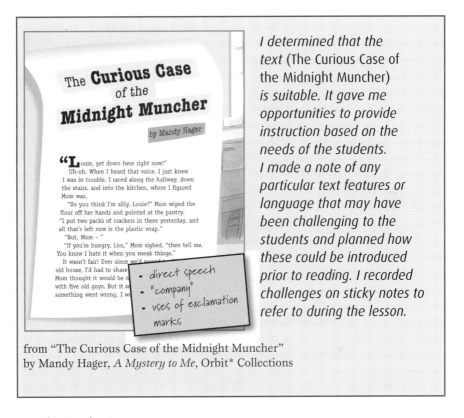

I determined that the text (The Curious Case of the Midnight Muncher) is suitable. It gave me opportunities to provide instruction based on the needs of the students. I made a note of any particular text features or language that may have been challenging to the students and planned how these could be introduced prior to reading. I recorded challenges on sticky notes to refer to during the lesson.

from "The Curious Case of the Midnight Muncher" by Mandy Hager, *A Mystery to Me*, Orbit* Collections

Introducing the text

When the group comes together, the teacher introduces the text by making deliberate links between the students' prior knowledge and the content, the overall theme, topic, or message, and the text structure. This is to ensure that the students are prepared for reading both the content and the structure.

This is a narrative text about a boy whose mother blames him for stealing food from the kitchen at night. But it isn't really him at all. He decides to find out who it is. From what you already know about the structure of a narrative text, what features would you expect to find in this story? Have you, or has someone you know, tried to prove that you are innocent of something you have been accused of? How determined would you be to clear your name? What words might we expect to encounter in a story about food going missing from the kitchen?

The learning goal is shared and the success criteria for the lesson are determined.

We are learning to use words in the text to help us infer what the author means as we read.

By the end of this lesson we will be able to find clues to help us figure out how Louie is feeling about the midnight muncher.

We will be successful when:
> *we have read the sections of text and thought about how Louie would be feeling*
> *we have found clues that help us figure out how Louie feels. These clues might be:*
> *– a word*
> *– a phrase*
> *– a piece of punctuation*
> *we are able to think about what the clues might mean and can relate them to our own experiences*
> *we share our clues and what we think they mean with others.*

The teacher discusses any unusual text features and ensures any possible challenges are resolved. This includes introducing important vocabulary that students may not know.

Reading and discussing the text

Students are asked to read a section of text (usually one or two paragraphs). They are given a specific purpose for their reading.

> *I want you to begin by reading the first twelve lines of the text (down to "You know I hate it when you sneak things.") Read to find out why Mom is talking to Louie.*

The students read the section of text independently. This is followed by discussion about the reading. The first question is typically related to the purpose the students were asked to read the section for.

> > *Why is Mom talking to Louie? What is he being accused of? How do you know this?*
> > *Does anyone have a different answer?*
> > *How do you know this is correct? What part of the text tells us this?*

Then the teacher and the students explore the content, text features, and challenges encountered in this section. This is where discussion will focus on developing the students' knowledge of inference.

> *We've got the sense that something is going missing. Are we actually told this or do we have to infer it?*

> *Louie feels that he is being blamed? Does Mom actually blame him or do we have to infer this?*

> *What words or phrases have you used to help you infer?*

> *Has punctuation helped us to infer?*

> *How? (Here I create opportunities for talking about the author's use of punctuation in portraying inference.)*

The teacher and students use the focus strategy to help comprehend the text. Together they look for where the author has used specific techniques to convey meaning, such as indirect references. The teacher will demonstrate and explain this to the students. Students may also be asked to demonstrate and explain their learning to one another. The teacher probes understanding by asking students for clarification and evidence to support their responses. Where possible, the teacher will give students responsibility for asking questions of the text and of one another.

At the conclusion of this discussion, a second section is assigned for independent reading. The teacher provides a purpose for this reading – it may be a question to think about, a prediction to test, or vocabulary to figure out. The students read this independently.

We know Mom is not happy with Louie. I wonder how Louie feels. Read the next two paragraphs to find out how he is feeling.

Silent reading is followed by discussion. Through discussion, questioning, and responding, the teacher ensures that students are gaining the overall meaning, and are also involved in learning about and practicing the focus strategy. The teacher directs the students' attention to where they need to use the strategy and uses the think-aloud approach to model how he or she used the strategy.

> *The author states that Louie is blamed for stealing more things from the kitchen. I noticed his first reaction was "It wasn't fair!" so I didn't think he was happy. He also doesn't seem happy about the others living in his house. I thought calling them a "bunch of boarders" showed he did not really like them, especially his use of the word "company" – this shows they are not really company for him. There is a sense that he feels he is blamed unfairly. I think that because of the way he says "every time something went wrong, I was blamed."*

Where students have difficulty recognizing or understanding a word, the teacher pauses to provide instruction (refer to chapters 2 and 3) and makes a mental note to include this as part of the follow-up students do in response to the lesson. If pausing is likely to be time-consuming or to detract from the main discussion, the teacher may choose to tell the students the word, recording it for instructional purposes at a later time.

> *The word Matthew is unsure of is "disappeared." This word comes from the root word "appear," which means visible or seen. The prefix "dis-" means "lack of" or "not." Put together, this means not visible, not seen.*

Usually this discussion is oral, but students may also be given a small written task to do in response to the reading.

> *Use your notebooks to record the key vocabulary the author has used to help you infer how Louie is feeling about being blamed for the missing food.*

At this stage, the teacher will try to lead the group from question and answer into a conversation about the reading. The teacher is constantly using questioning and discussion to check on the students comprehension of the text.

A third section of text is assigned for reading, and the procedure continues. The procedure includes:

- reading a section of text for a specific purpose
- discussion, conversation, and questioning around text content and the author's use of implied meaning
- opportunities for teachers to use the think-aloud approach to draw students' attention to examples where they need to infer meaning
- opportunities for students to talk about and demonstrate their own understanding to others
- opportunities for students to question others and get feedback from their peers.

As the lesson progresses, the teacher will ask questions aimed to assess the students' developing understanding of the text, questions that require the students to support their responses and explain the comprehension strategies they are using. The teacher and students will also revisit the success criteria throughout the lesson to see whether they are achieving them. Where the teacher detects that students are having difficulty, he or she will adjust instruction accordingly.

A follow-up task that relates to the learning goals may be set for students to complete either as a group, in pairs, or on their own. This task should be designed to build on the learning achieved in the lesson.

Reflecting on practice

An observation guide to support reading comprehension instruction through guided reading is provided in appendix 6.2 (page 245). Teachers can use this as described on page 212.

Reciprocal reading

What is reciprocal reading?

Reciprocal reading is a small-group instructional reading approach initially developed by Palinscar and Brown (1984) to explicitly focus student attention on four reading comprehension strategies. These strategies are:

- asking questions
- clarifying what was read
- summarizing information
- predicting what might follow.

As with guided and shared reading, this approach includes the teacher as a member of the group, modeling, explaining, questioning, and using the think-aloud approach to make comprehension strategies visible and to show how they can be used to make meaning from a wide variety of texts.

Reciprocal reading is a sound approach to use with older students and across the curriculum. It can help students understand how to read like a scientist, a mathematician, or a historian.

The aim of this teaching approach is to develop students' metacognitive thinking through discussing the comprehension strategies they use with their peers. As the students become more confident at using this approach, the teacher steps aside from leading the group to become one of the group members. The students take over leadership of the group and the role of supporting others as they read. This approach uses the principles of metacognitive comprehension instruction (described in chapter 1) to gradually increase students' active engagement in their own learning.

Teachers will find it useful to preteach each of the four strategies. This can be done effectively through a series of mini-lessons or through a shared reading lesson. It is not necessary for students to be expert at using the strategies before they start reciprocal reading because participating in the approach will help them to develop their ability with each strategy. The aim of preteaching is familiarization with each strategy so that students are able to participate in reciprocal reading from the outset. *See also the descriptions of these strategies in chapter 5.*

The teacher introduces the text or text excerpt to the students, ensuring that they have enough prior knowledge to cope with the content and text structure, then sets the first section to be read (for example, one or two paragraphs).

The students and teacher read the assigned section silently. After reading it, the teacher initiates a discussion based on the four reciprocal reading strategies. These strategies (and prompts for using them) are often written onto cards for students to refer to.

When the discussion is completed, the teacher assigns the next section of text and the procedure continues.

The Reciprocal Reading Procedure

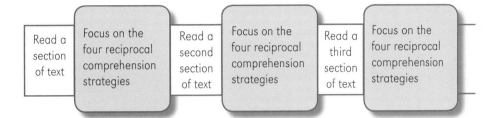

As the students become comfortable with the strategies and the discussion format, the teacher assigns students to specific roles. These are:

Group leader – the leader facilitates the session, prompts for responses as needed, and keeps the session moving. The leader also directs the reading by telling the group how far to read for each section.

Clarifier, questioner, summarizer, predictor – at the end of each section of text, students take responsibility for discussing one of the strategies. Their role is to respond to the strategy, then ask for discussion or suggestions from other group members. One student will take responsibility for clarifying, one for questioning, one for summarizing, and one for predicting.

At the end of each discussion, the roles rotate, so each member of the group has a turn at leading discussion on at least one of the four strategies, depending on the length of the text and the number of students in the group.

This approach can be used with groups of four to eight students. When there are more students than roles, those without a specific role are still involved in the discussion. When roles are changed after each section of text, all students have the chance to lead discussion on the strategies.

The students will usually need a period of direct instruction to learn how to use the approach so that they will eventually be able to manage the process with minimal supervision. A fishbowl technique can be used for this instruction, with the reading group in the middle and other students observing. As the students gradually take over responsibility, the teacher monitors the use of the approach carefully to ensure that it works smoothly and that the discussions are focused and go beyond a literal interpretation of the text.

Reciprocal reading strategies

The four strategies in this approach are:

1. Clarifying
2. Questioning
3. Summarizing
4. Predicting.

Clarifying

This strategy is about making the author's message clear to the reader. Clarifying statements involve students asking:

- Something I am not sure about is ...
- A word I need clarifying is ...
- Can someone help me clarify ...?
- An idea I need clarified is ...

Questioning

This strategy encourages students to build their understanding by asking questions of the text and of the author's intentions. Students may say:

- A question I have is ...
- Can someone tell me why ...?
- My question is ...
- I have been wondering why ...

Summarizing

This strategy supports students to summarize what has been read. It helps the students to separate the relevant information from unimportant details and assists them to organize information from consecutive paragraphs.

- This section has been about ...
- A summary of this passage is ...
- The main events so far have been ...
- The most important point the author made was ...

Predicting

Using this strategy, the students use all the available information to make a prediction about what they think will follow. Students may say:

- As we read the next section, I predict ... because ...
- I predict the next section will be about ... because ...
- I predict ... will happen in the next paragraph because ...

Using the reciprocal reading approach to support learning

In this section, we go "inside" a reciprocal reading lesson to see how students develop a metacognitive awareness of the strategies and their uses. Note that in this description, we assume that the students are already familiar with reciprocal reading strategies and are beginning to take a leadership role in the lesson.

Inside the reciprocal reading lesson

Planning the lesson

The teacher has gathered data to determine the students' learning needs.

Ms. Hales identified that several students have difficulty in comprehending factual text. They are not confident in reading material to support their social studies or science knowledge and find it difficult to locate, discuss, and summarize the most important material. They are also often confused by subject-specific vocabulary and the use of technical terms. Her analysis will affect:

a. text selection – the teaching will focus on a variety of factual texts that support topics studied in class

b. the role of the teacher – from leader to supporter as students become more confident in using reciprocal approaches to comprehend factual text

c. the type of follow-up activities that the teacher will set at the conclusion of the lesson and in preparation for subsequent lessons.

The teacher selects an appropriate text and ensures that the materials needed for the lesson are ready. This will include a copy of the text for each student, a dictionary, and a variety of reference materials, such as informational books, maps, encyclopedias, and access to computer reference tools. If the teacher wants students to write or draw responses, they will need to have individual whiteboards, paper, or notebooks.

The teacher may prepare a set of cards to support the strategy use during the session.

Sectioning the text

During planning, the teacher reads the text and makes decisions about suitable places to divide it for reading. These decisions will depend on the students' needs and the difficulty of the text. Sectioning the text will eventually become the responsibility of the group leader.

Introducing the text

The teacher introduces the text, making deliberate links between the content and the area of study. This could be a social studies or science topic, a procedure or word problem in mathematics, or a literature study. The learning goal and success criteria for the lesson are shared with the students.

During our study we are learning what causes natural disasters and the effect these have on families and communities. The text we are going to read is about a tsunami. A tsunami is a natural disaster. This text will tell us what tsunamis are and how they occur.

We are using reciprocal reading to learn to:
> *identify the main facts the author is telling us*
> *practice using subject-specific vocabulary to explain and talk about the main facts*
> *practice the strategies of clarifying, questioning, summarizing, and predicting to help us understand factual text.*

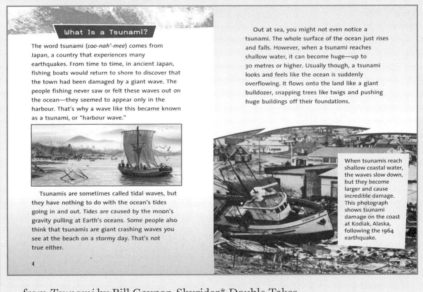

What Is a Tsunami?

The word tsunami (*soo-nah'-mee*) comes from Japan, a country that experiences many earthquakes. From time to time, in ancient Japan, fishing boats would return to shore to discover that the town had been damaged by a giant wave. The people fishing never saw or felt these waves out on the ocean—they seemed to appear only in the harbour. That's why a wave like this became known as a tsunami, or "harbour wave."

Tsunamis are sometimes called tidal waves, but they have nothing to do with the ocean's tides going in and out. Tides are caused by the moon's gravity pulling at Earth's oceans. Some people also think that tsunamis are giant crashing waves you see at the beach on a stormy day. That's not true either.

4

Out at sea, you might not even notice a tsunami. The whole surface of the ocean just rises and falls. However, when a tsunami reaches shallow water, it can become huge—up to 30 metres or higher. Usually though, a tsunami looks and feels like the ocean is suddenly overflowing. It flows onto the land like a giant bulldozer, snapping trees like twigs and pushing huge buildings off their foundations.

When tsunamis reach shallow coastal water, the waves slow down, but they become larger and cause incredible damage. This photograph shows tsunami damage on the coast at Kodiak, Alaska, following the 1964 earthquake.

from *Tsunami* by Bill Gaynor, Skyrider* Double Takes

Reading and discussing the text

The teacher (or later, the leader) sets the first section to be read. The students read this section to themselves. When the students have finished reading, four students each take up a role, using the four cards as guides.

Clarifying

The clarifier asks a question to clarify something in the text. The question may relate to all or part of the section. The students share their ideas and refer to the text to support them. If the students are not sure or if the responses are off-track or incorrect, the teacher may refer the group to a reference text and explain the point to the group. The leader then asks the group if anyone else has something they would like to have clarified before moving to the second strategy.

> Jamie is the clarifier:
> *I would like some help to clarify what exactly a tsunami is.*

Questioning

The questioner asks a question about what they have just read, and the students share their responses. The teacher monitors the responses and adds suggestions as appropriate. If the students are unable to answer the question or if their ideas are confused, the teacher gives an answer and uses the think-aloud approach to show the thinking that led to the answer. The leader then checks to see if anyone else has a question before the group moves to the third strategy.

> Luis is the questioner:
> *A question I have is why does the author say a tsunami looks and feels like the sea is suddenly overflowing?*

Summarizing

The summarizer gives a brief summary of the section and checks with the group to see if the summary is accurate. Discussion may arise as students respond with their own summaries. The teacher supports the group as they agree on a summary before moving on to the fourth strategy.

> George is the summarizer:
> *My summary from what I have read so far is this: tsunamis are large waves that only occur and cause damage in a harbor, not out at sea. This is because they become huge when they reach shallow water and cause vast damage to coastal land.*

Predicting

The predictor makes a prediction about what he or she might read in the next section, giving a reason for the prediction. The group discusses the prediction.

> Bella is the predictor:
> *The next section is titled an eye witness account. Therefore, I predict that this section will tell us exactly what it is like to be in a tsunami by someone who has experienced one.*

Handing over responsibility

As the group becomes more confident at using the approach, the teacher may gradually hand over most of the responsibility for managing the process and leading the discussion. Ultimately, the group leader will direct the reading as the teacher monitors progress, supporting the leader's decisions with feedback. In this way, the teacher is able to link the work of the group to the formative assessment process.

The group is then assigned a further section of text to read (one to three paragraphs), and the cycle starts again. The students' roles are changed so that different students have responsibility for each role. This can be done by handing the card on to the next person in the group.

The procedure continues as students read their way through the text.

Reflecting on practice

An observation guide to support reading comprehension instruction using the reciprocal reading teaching approach is provided in appendix 6.3 (page 247) as described on page 212.

Supporting instructional approaches

The following section outlines four other instructional approaches that can be used with reading comprehension instruction to supplement the main approaches of shared, guided, and reciprocal reading within the instructional comprehension program (refer to the diagram on page 202). The approaches discussed are:

- Questioning the author
- Literature circles
- Repeated paired reading
- Readers' theater.

Questioning the author

Questioning the author, identified as a reading comprehension teaching approach by researchers Beck, McKeown, Hamilton, and Kucan, (1997), encourages students' dialogue with the author to build and strengthen comprehension. By asking questions of the author, students are encouraged to think about who wrote the text, the purpose for writing it, and the intended audience. The approach is particularly effective for developing inference because the students are not actually in contact with the author: they must infer the author's purpose and meaning by careful reading of the text.

Asking questions of the author also helps students to focus on the important components of a text and to discuss ideas and interpretations of a text. Questioning the author is useful in teaching students how to ask questions before, during, and after reading, and links to the comprehension strategy of asking and answering questions (see chapter 5).

In this approach, students read selected sections of text. After reading each section, the students ask questions related to author's purpose and meaning. The nature of the questions depends on the needs of the students and the kind of text they are reading.

For example, if students are trying to determine the author's point of view, they may ask questions that include:

- What is the author trying to convince me of?
- Why is the author doing this?
- How does the author convey a point of view?

Sometimes questions are recorded on charts and used as prompts. As students read sections of text, they stop to ask questions of the author, to reread the text for clues and answers, and to discuss the questions and possible answers. In this way, they also develop the ability to think critically about text. Through the processes of questioning the author, students learn to ask their own questions of text. The questions they ask may be focused on a variety of purposes that include:

- to create meaning
- to relate what they have read to their own experiences
- to improve understanding
- to find answers – literal and inferential
- to solve problems
- to learn something new
- to learn about the author's purpose
- to critically analyze a text.

These purposes could be listed on a chart for reference.

Literature circles

Literature circles (Daniels, 1994) are most often used when students are reading novels. They are similar to the kind of book discussion clubs that adults may belong to. Students select a book to read, at first with guidance from the teacher if necessary. These are sometimes recreational and sometimes around a theme (for example, a history or social studies theme may be supported by a series of novels set in a particular time or place). Students form groups based on the books they are reading. They meet regularly to discuss their text and share notes, diagrams, discussion questions, and drawings. When students finish reading one text, they form new groups based on their new choices.

Literature circles are an effective way of encouraging students to read independently and for pleasure. Students can also be assigned various roles within the literature circles. These roles include:

- Discussion leader – this student's role is to ask open-ended questions and to facilitate discussion by group members.
- Illustrator – this student's role is to sketch key scenes from the text and to encourage dialogue among group members about the events in these scenes.
- Literature detective – this student brings key excerpts from the text to share and discuss. This may be a piece with challenging or interesting vocabulary, an explicit description, or a piece that the student found difficult. The literature detective should be prepared to share the excerpt and the reason for its selection with other group members.
- Vocabulary enricher – this student sources and presents definitions for unusual or new vocabulary in the text.
- Connector – this student looks for relationships among what the students are reading, their own experiences, and events in the world. They may also make connections with other books that the group has read, for example, books by the same author.
- Investigator – this student looks for background information related to the text and brings this information to share with the group.

Roles can vary from meeting to meeting, with students choosing or being assigned a role for the next meeting at the end of each session. Sharing roles is an effective way of engaging students in text.

Repeated paired reading

Repeated reading (Samuels, 1997) provides students with many opportunities to engage with a text. Often on the first reading of a text, there are many challenges for students to overcome. They may encounter unknown words, or new concepts or ideas. The challenges can also be a combination of these. For this reason, repeating the reading a number of times for different purposes is useful in developing word knowledge and comprehension of text.

At a simpler level, repeated reading provides opportunities for students to practice specific strategies to support their comprehension and to develop confidence in their use.

Repeated reading with a partner has the additional benefit of providing an audience for reading and a partner to discuss the reading. When students undertake repeated reading with a partner, they can practice the think-aloud approach to explain the strategies they are using and why they used them. They can also set and answer questions for one another. Partners can provide one another with feedback on their reading that is related to a particular goal. As with the other approaches, students will need to have this explained and modeled carefully by the teacher before responsibility is gradually handed over. The fishbowl method (see page 227) is an effective way of showing and practicing how to give and receive feedback between peers.

Example 1

Students are engaged in repeated paired reading with a focus on providing feedback to one another on the use of fluency behaviors in oral reading. One partner reads a section, and the listener provides feedback.

Example 2

Students are engaged in repeated paired reading with a focus on practicing the strategy of making connections between their reading and their prior knowledge. Students have been taught that making connections to prior knowledge is an important strategy because it teaches them to relate newly learned information to things they already know so that they can improve their overall knowledge and understanding. As they read, they stop to question one another – What do we already know? What do we now know? What are we learning from this text?

Readers' theater

Readers' theater (Bidwell, 1990; Dixon, et. al., 1996) can be used for a text that has already been used in guided or shared reading. It provides opportunities for students to practice oral reading and thus develop fluency, accuracy, and intonation (see also chapter 4). It is based on research that shows the benefits of repeated reading by providing opportunities for second, third, and fourth readings through which students build their knowledge of vocabulary and increase their comprehension. It is most suitable for narrative texts that contain enough dialogue and action to make the text a challenge and can involve several students as characters. As well as practicing reading strategies, readers' theater gives students opportunities to develop their speaking and listening skills.

from "Eating Snow" by Feana Tuʻakoi, Power Zone* *Lost? Found!*

The approach requires students to use the text as a script with "parts" for the characters in the story. A part can be assigned to a narrator who reads the narrative parts of the text that cannot be given through dialogue. The script is most easily created by giving the students photocopies of the text and asking them to highlight the "parts" that they will read. Rewriting the text as a script is not usually advised because it takes the focus away from reading and comprehending the text as originally written.

The students practice reading their parts aloud, working through difficult words together to improve fluency and comprehension. They also practice how to emphasize the most important messages. After several practices, the students present the script to others. There are no scenes or actions in the presentation, only voices that are assigned to different readers. The emphasis for the readers is on the tone, pace, phrasing, intonation, and emphasis to give an interpretation that the audience can imagine.

Readers' theater can be adapted in various ways, but the following steps provide a guide to its use within the context of reading comprehension. Readers' theater can be used as a follow-up to a shared, guided, or reciprocal reading session.

- A narrative text (or section of text) that has previously been read by students is selected.
- Students reread the text and discuss the key roles and events.
- Students are assigned roles or parts to read.
- Students practice reading their roles.
- Students come together and practice reading the text, taking responsibility for their roles.
- Several rehearsal readings occur, then students present the theater.
- The group discusses how they used their oral reading and their knowledge of the text to show the underlying meaning to their audience.

Summary

This chapter has described a number of instructional approaches that can be used to enhance metacognition and thus raise the reading comprehension abilities of students. While the approaches in this chapter are not intended to be an exhaustive list, each approach (when modified and developed to meet the specific needs of students) has been shown to be effective in developing reading comprehension ability.

It is important for teachers to use the approaches selectively, to plan lessons to meet the needs of their students, and to use the principles of metacognitive comprehension instruction as outlined in chapter 1: this includes using formative assessment practices so that (as well as giving the teacher essential information for planning) the students know what they are learning and their progress in learning.

When students have difficulty comprehending a text, lessons are modified to respond to these difficulties. In this way, each approach can be used to provide an appropriate balance of content, vocabulary, word level, and strategy teaching.

References and recommended reading

Allen, J. (2002). *On the Same Page: Shared Reading Beyond the Primary Grades.* Portland, Maine: Stenhouse.

Beck, I. L., McKeown, M. G., Hamilton, R. L., and Kucan, L. (1997). *Questioning the Author: An Approach for Enhancing Student Engagement with Text.* Newark, Delaware: International Reading Association.

Bidwell, S. M. (1990). "Using Drama to Increase Motivation, Comprehension, and Fluency". *Journal of Reading,* 34, pp. 38–41.

Brown, S. (2004). *Shared Reading for Grades 3 and Beyond: Working It Out Together.* Wellington, New Zealand: Learning Media.

Clay, M. M. (1991). *Becoming Literate: The Construction of Inner Control.* Portsmouth, New Hampshire: Heinemann.

Daniels, H. (1994). *Literature Circles: Voice and Choice in the Student-Centered Classroom.* York, Maine: Stenhouse.

Dixon, N., Davies, A., and Politano, C. (1996). *Learning with Readers' Theatre: Building Connections.* Winnipeg, Holdaway: Peguis.

Expert Panel on Literacy in Grades 4 to 6 in Ontario (2004). *Literacy for Learning: The Report of the Expert Panel on Literacy in Grades 4 to 6 in Ontario.* Ontario Ministry of Education.

Fountas, I. and Pinnell, G. S. (2001). *Guiding Readers and Writers (Grades 3–6): Teaching Comprehension, Genre, and Content Literacy.* Portsmouth, New Hampshire: Heinemann.

Holdaway, D. (1979). *The Foundations of Literacy.* Exeter, New Hampshire: Heinemann.

Ministry of Education (2003). *Effective Literacy Practice in Years 1 to 4.* Wellington, New Zealand: Learning Media.

Ministry of Education (2004). *Guided Reading in Years 5 to 8.* Wellington, New Zealand: Learning Media.

Ministry of Education (2005). *Effective Literacy Practice in Years 5 to 8.* Wellington, New Zealand: Learning Media.

Mooney, M. (1988). *Developing Life-long Readers.* Wellington, New Zealand: Department of Education.

Palinscar, A. S. and Brown, A. L. (1984). "Reciprocal Teaching of Comprehension-fostering and Comprehension-monitoring Activities". *Cognition and Instruction,* 1, pp. 117–175.

Pressley, M. (2006). *Reading Instruction That Works: The Case for Balanced Teaching.* (3rd ed.) New York, New York: The Guilford Press.

Rog, L. J. (2003). *Guided Reading Basics: Organizing, Managing, and Implementing a Balanced Literacy Program in K–3.* Portland, Maine: Stenhouse.

Samuels, S. J. (1997). "The Method of Repeated Readings". *The Reading Teacher,* 50, pp. 376–381 (original work published in 1979).

APPENDIX 6.1

Shared reading reflection or observation guide

Planning the lesson

- The purpose of the lesson is clear in the teacher's mind. **Yes/No**
- The teacher has read the text prior to the lesson, sectioned the text if necessary, and has identified key teaching points and/or questions for each section. **Yes/No**
- The student achievement data (from previous lessons and from assessment) has been used to inform the selection of text, the key teaching points, and the learning goals. **Yes/No**

Comments

Introducing the text

- The learning goals are shared in writing with the students. **Yes/No**
- The teacher has explained these, discussing them with the students so that they understand what they mean. **Yes/No**
- The success criteria are shared with students. (Teachers may now be involving students in establishing the success criteria.) **Yes/No**
- The theme, main idea, purpose, or topic of the text is made explicit to the students. **Yes/No**
- The teacher deliberately makes connections to students' prior knowledge and experience of the theme, key idea, topic, or purpose to prepare them for the context of the reading. **Yes/No**

Students may have been engaged in an activity to connect with their prior knowledge before the lesson. This may have been a KWL activity, a graphic organizer, a brainstorm, an oral group discussion with key questions, or a prediction based on some of the illustrations in the text. Where this has occurred, the teacher will ask students to share their expectations of the text at the introduction of the lesson – gaining information on what the students know on the theme, topic, main idea, or purpose of what is to be read and what possible challenge students may have as a result of this.

Comments

Reading and discussing the text

- The teacher sets the first section and a purpose for the reading.   **Yes/No**
- The teacher reads the first section aloud.   **Yes/No**
- The students follow the teacher, reading along silently or aloud.   **Yes/No**

After the teacher reads aloud, there is questioning and discussion where:

- The teacher asks clear questions and allows time for student responses. (The teacher does not answer the questions, move on too quickly, or ask another question before the first is completed.)   **Yes/No**
- The students are encouraged to respond to the answers of their peers, often prompted by the teacher. This is important in leading toward a discussion of the text, rather than a question and answer session.   **Yes/No**
- Any key vocabulary is discussed with the students.   **Yes/No**

As necessary, teachers may take a short mini-lesson before moving on to the next section (for example, around a key idea, phrase, or unknown word). Teachers may also make use of the think, pair, share strategy to engage students in discussion around the text.

- Sectioning, setting a purpose for the section, and follow-up discussion of the text continues through the reading.   **Yes/No**
- The students are encouraged to ask questions of the text.   **Yes/No**
- The learning goal is revisited as the lesson progresses. (It is referred to throughout the lesson, not just at the beginning and end of the lesson.)   **Yes/No**

Comments

Lesson conclusion

- Key ideas from the text and discussion are summarized.   **Yes/No**
- The learning goal is revisited with the students.   **Yes/No**
- The success criteria are revisited with the students.   **Yes/No**
- Students are involved in self-assessing how well they progressed toward meeting the criteria.   **Yes/No**
- A follow-up task is set that relates to either further reading of the text or the learning goal and success criteria set for this lesson.   **Yes/No**

Note: It is very important that the follow-up task relates to and builds on student learning. The teacher and the students should be able to tell you how this is so.

Comments

Follow-up tasks

- The purpose of any follow-up task is clear to all students.   **Yes/No**
- The purpose of the follow-up task relates to the learning outcome set for the lesson.   **Yes/No**

Summary of reflection or observation

Features of the lesson that worked particularly well

Areas for future support

(suggestions for a personal professional development goal that arose from the observations)

APPENDIX 6.2

Guided reading reflection or observation guide

Planning the lesson

- The purpose of the lesson is clear in the teacher's mind. **Yes/No**
- The text matches the students' reading level and interests. **Yes/No**
- The teacher has read the text prior to the lesson, sectioned the text, and has identified key teaching points and questions for each section. **Yes/No**
- The student achievement data (from previous lessons and from assessment) has been used to inform the selection of the text, the key teaching points, and the learning goals. **Yes/No**

Introducing the text

- The lesson goal and success criteria have been shared with the students. **Yes/No**
- The teacher has introduced the text or topic and related the main theme or key ideas to the students' prior knowledge. **Yes/No**
- Any unusual features or possible challenges (for example, in vocabulary or text structure) are shared and explained to the students. **Yes/No**

Comments

Reading and discussing the text

- The teacher sets the purpose for reading each section of text. (for example, "I want you to read to find out ...") **Yes/No**
- The students read the text themselves. (Fluent students are encouraged to read silently.) **Yes/No**
- Discussion is focused and related to the lesson goal. There will be questions and answers leading to in-depth discussion – the teacher will try to use a variety of rich questions ensuring that not all questions are closed. In this way, the discussion may explore text features, key ideas, and identified challenges. **Yes/No**

- The teacher probes the students' understanding, asking for clarification, reasons why, evidence from the text, and other ideas. **Yes/No**
- The students are encouraged to think and talk about what they are reading. **Yes/No**

Comments

Lesson conclusion

- The purpose (learning goal) of the lesson is revisited. **Yes/No**
- The students reflect on what they have learned. **Yes/No**
- The teacher provides opportunities for further reading. **Yes/No**
- Any follow-up activities are related to the learning goal and success criteria shared at the beginning of the lesson. **Yes/No**

Comments

Follow-up tasks

- The purpose of any follow-up task is clear to all students. **Yes/No**
- The purpose of the follow-up task relates to the learning goal set for the lesson. **Yes/No**

Summary of reflection or observation

Features of the lesson that worked particularly well

Areas for future support

(suggestions for a personal professional development goal that arose from the observations)

APPENDIX 6.3

Reciprocal reading reflection or observation guide

Planning the lesson

· The purpose of the lesson is clear in the teacher's mind.	**Yes/No**
· The text matches the students' reading level and interests.	**Yes/No**
· The teacher has read the text prior to the lesson, sectioned the text, and has identified key teaching points and questions for each role.	**Yes/No**
· The student achievement data (from previous lessons and from assessment) has been used to inform the selection of text, the key teaching points, and the learning goals.	**Yes/No**

Comments

Introducing the text

At this stage, the teacher should introduce the text to the students and share the learning goal. Text content is what the text is about; text type is the type of text (narrative, report, etc.). Learning goals and success criteria should be written down so that they can be referred to as the lesson develops. Learning goals start: "We are learning to ..." Success criteria indicate: "We will be successful if we can ..."

· The text content is introduced to the students.	**Yes/No**
· The text type is introduced to the students.	**Yes/No**
· The learning goal is written for the students.	**Yes/No**
· The success criteria are written for the students.	**Yes/No**
· The students were aware of the purpose of the lesson prior to reading.	**Yes/No**

Comments

Reading and discussing the text

At this stage, the students begin reciprocal reading. The text is divided into sections to be read and discussed. The students have specific roles – these roles should be written on index cards and the students should be following them. As the lesson progresses, the roles within the group will change. At first, the teacher is leading the roles and participating to ensure that the level of discussion and interaction with text is high.

- Reciprocal reading roles are written on card for the students to follow.   **Yes/No**
- The students are able to ask for clarification of unknown words.   **Yes/No**
- The students are able to ask for clarification of unknown concepts.   **Yes/No**
- The students are able to ask questions from the text.   **Yes/No**
- The students are able to predict.   **Yes/No**
- The students are able to give reasons for their predictions.   **Yes/No**
- The students are able to summarize.   **Yes/No**
- The teacher provides support when necessary.   **Yes/No**
- The teacher actively encourages a high level of discussion as the session progresses.   **Yes/No**

Comments

Lesson conclusion

- The teacher revisits the lesson goal.   **Yes/No**
- The teacher asks the students what they learned.   **Yes/No**
- The teacher refers the students to the success criteria.   **Yes/No**
- The teacher checks new learning of each student to determine areas of future need.   **Yes/No**

Comments

Follow-up tasks

- The purpose of the follow-up task is clear to all the students.   **Yes/No**
- The purpose of the follow-up task relates to the learning goal
  set for the lesson.   **Yes/No**

Summary of reflection or observation

Features of the lesson that worked particularly well

Areas for future support

(suggestions for a personal professional development goal that arose from the observations)

Working with Groups

While heterogeneous groupings are often used in grades 3 to 8, the most effective comprehension instruction occurs with small, relatively homogeneous groups of students to ensure the best fit between instruction and the students' needs. Teachers will also work with the class as a whole (for example, reading aloud, some shared reading, text and topic discussions), but specific, focused comprehension instruction is most effective in a group setting. This chapter gives practical advice on establishing and maintaining a reading program using group-based instruction.

Key messages for teachers

- Students are grouped for metacognitive comprehension instruction based on similar reading levels and/or learning needs.

- Routines are taught and established to support the organization and management of group work within the classroom.

- Groups change as the year progresses and the needs of students change.

- Student learning can be practiced, reinforced, maintained, and extended through follow-up lessons with the teacher.

Group-based instruction allows teachers to think about the needs of specific groups of students and to plan a program aimed at meeting those needs. It provides a way of ensuring that all students participate actively in lessons. When students receive instruction in small groups (for example, six to eight students) they can't easily hide from the teacher's attention or from participating with their peers.

Group-based instruction

There are many ways to group students in grades 3 to 8 and many excellent reasons for using mixed groupings. For the purpose of metacognitive comprehension instruction, however, students are best grouped according to similar reading abilities and/or instructional needs.

Not all students need the same instructional focus, not all students are able to read the same text, and not all students will be sufficiently challenged by the same text. They will certainly not all be ready to read the same text at the same time.

Group-based instruction ensures that the instruction will be more likely to meet the students' needs rather than be "hit and miss." While few teachers would consciously deliver hit-and-miss instruction, the reality is that students have different needs and one-size-fits-all lessons are not likely to meet those needs. This is particularly true for instruction to develop reading comprehension. By dividing the class into manageable groups of similar ability, teachers are more able to select texts and learning goals to match the actual learning needs of the student.

Group instruction enables teachers to work in-depth on a text with a few students at a time. This means that the teacher and the students can more easily be involved in the process of making meaning. There is opportunity for every student to respond to questions, to find evidence to support their responses, to ask questions of the text and of one another, and to focus their learning on the strategies to make meaning from text.

Teachers are better able to monitor the progress of each student when they are working in small groups. They do this by questioning the strategies the students use to understand a text, responding to the students' questions about the text, and responding to the students' questions about their understanding. Within these interactions, each student's progress and future needs become apparent to the teacher. The teacher gathers valuable information from the students contributions and from their ability to achieve the goals for the lesson.

Group instruction ensures a consistent degree of engagement and on-task performance. Because students are working in a small group and the activity is appropriate to their level, teachers find that there is less disruption and a higher degree of engagement. This is especially so when students are aware of the purpose, when they are involved in setting the learning goals and success criteria, and when learning strategies are made explicit to them.

Lev Vygotsky's widely accepted theory about learning suggests that optimal learning occurs when the teacher determines a student's level of understanding and teaches at an appropriate level of challenge to lead the student toward independence (Vygotsky, 1978). By working with small groups who have similar instructional needs, teachers can deliver instruction that is appropriate to each group.

Establishing groups

Students are constantly building onto prior learning, so their needs will change over time. A group that was once relatively homogeneous may change when some students pick up a new strategy more quickly than others or when the learning goals change. Teachers plan to establish groups with the information they have at the start of the year, then reform the groups as needs change.

Grouping at the start of the school year

At the beginning of the year, teachers will often receive information on student achievement from previous teachers. This may be a portfolio of work, including samples of tests and guided reading level information, spelling and writing samples, and records of oral reading. All information needs to be questioned carefully:

- What does information from the previous year indicate about the student's strengths and learning needs?
- What achievement level did the student reach the previous year?
- What progress was made in the previous year?
- Did the student receive any extra or special support in previous years?

It is also important for teachers to check that any assessment information is a fair measure of their students' strengths and needs. Teachers may need to find out more by asking:

- Does this match the other information I have on this student?
- Does this confirm what I already know?
- Are there any surprises in this information?
- What other information do I need to gather? (for example, talk to the student about what makes reading difficult or easy, observe the student during a lesson, ask the student whether he or she likes reading and why, use a second comprehension assessment tool to explore a particular aspect of learning)

Teachers may also receive results from a standardized reading comprehension test. It is extremely important for teachers to know what the test assesses if they are to use it to inform teaching and to group students. Often, groups of test items will assess specific skills, and this can help determine the direction of group instruction. Questions teachers often ask as they analyze these results include:

- What was this assessment requiring the students to do?
- What has the student been able to do?
- What errors has the student made? How often?
- What kinds of errors are they? What has caused these errors to occur? What trends are becoming evident?

Students for whom no information is available can be assessed using assessment activities such as those described in chapters 2, 3, 4, and 5 in conjunction with other commonly used school assessments.

As they analyze assessment information, teachers will consider what it will mean for the way they interact with their students, how they will motivate and engage their learners, and how they will plan to meet their instructional needs.

From this information, teachers will make decisions about grouping the students according to their learning needs and their levels of reading achievement. They identify the reading level and needs of the groups, prioritize learning goals, select suitable texts, and make decisions about the best teaching approaches.

Class Summary Sheet

Ms. Kelly, Room 314   Grade 4 [   ]

Student	Date	Level	Instructional needs	Comments
David	10/21	M	Self-monitoring for word recognition and understanding	Check word recognition strategies. Slow down and read for meaning — retelling focus.
Kristina	10/21	Q	Visualizing, asking questions	Use rich descriptive texts to embed strategies.
Jacob	10/22	T	Finding main ideas Synthesizing information across texts	Loves research but needs to hone skills
Jacinta	10/22	Q	Making and checking predictions	Develop confidence
Gretel	10/25	M	Word recognition: syllables, analogy	Needs daily focus on words; build background knowledge
Jorge	10/25	R	Distinguishing interesting from important ideas	
Tyler	10/28	N	Using own knowledge to predict	Build background knowledge

Group 1	Group 2	Group 3
David	Jacinta	Jorge
Gretel	Kristina	Alla
Susie		Laurie
Tyler		

Adjusting groups as the year progresses

While it is important the groups are established at the beginning of the year, they will likely change several times as the year progresses. Groups are only useful in meeting the needs of the students in them. When teachers match their teaching to the needs of their students, students will make progress. Therefore, teachers need to check on their group organization throughout the year and ask themselves whether, as a result of the rate of each student's progress and in light of achievement gains, they may need to reorganize groups.

Grouping should always be flexible. This involves:

- regular monitoring of the progress in each group. Sharing, assessing, and reflecting on the learning goals and success criteria provide an effective way of doing this in the course of the teaching program;
- adjusting groups according to progress made;
- drawing on formative assessment to assist decision making about group placement;
- making adjustments according to student interest on a topic or preference for a type of reading (for example, a preference for narrative or informational texts).

Formative assessment

This includes the use of formal and informal observations of students. It can be informal discussions between teachers and students; discussions during instructional lessons; interviews with students to determine areas of strength, need, interest, and motivation; analyzing student responses to independent and group comprehension activities; analyzing samples of completed work; gaining feedback from students and self-assessments; and reviewing student goal-setting tasks.

See also chapter 1 for further information about formative assessment.

Managing and organizing group-based instruction

Having placed students into groups for focused comprehension instruction, teachers plan exactly what they will be asking each group to do to meet the learning goals they have set. The lesson content will be determined by the goals, texts, and approaches the teacher has decided to use: see chapters 3, 4, and 5 for specific information about teaching to figure out words, develop vocabulary and fluency, and use comprehension strategies. Chapter 6 contains detailed information about the approaches that teachers can use to provide metacognitive comprehension instruction in small groups.

While the teacher works with one group, the other students need to be engaged in purposeful activities that relate directly to their learning goals and can be done independently. These form a cycle of prereading activity, reading instruction with the teacher, and post-reading activity. The cycle continues as the teacher selects new learning goals and new texts and sets suitable activities for each group.

Group-based instruction cycle

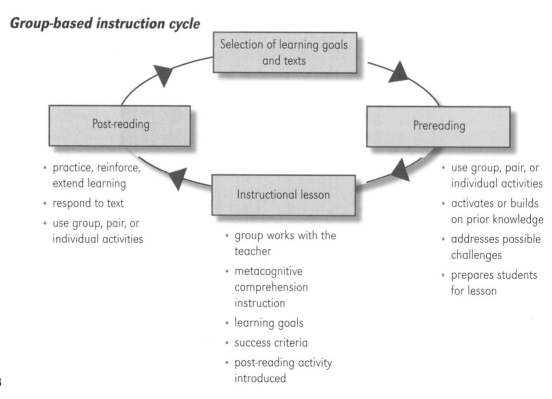

Selection of learning goals and texts

Post-reading
- practice, reinforce, extend learning
- respond to text
- use group, pair, or individual activities

Prereading
- use group, pair, or individual activities
- activates or builds on prior knowledge
- addresses possible challenges
- prepares students for lesson

Instructional lesson
- group works with the teacher
- metacognitive comprehension instruction
- learning goals
- success criteria
- post-reading activity introduced

Planning for those who are *not* with the teacher

As the diagram indicates, at any one time, one group of students will be working with the teacher while the other groups are engaged in pre or post-reading activities. These groups will be either preparing for a lesson or following-up from one. Any one group may have a lesson with the teacher every day or (more commonly) every second or third day. When they are not with the teacher, they will be working on their respective activities. An activity may take two or three days to complete.

The planning of high-quality activities for those who are not receiving direct instruction is just as important as planning for the lessons. To plan activities that will motivate and engage students, teachers will need to:

- draw on their knowledge of the students to determine key learning goals for each group;
- select appropriate texts for each group for a one or two week time frame. The texts will be selected because they match the learning needs of students, contain interesting and appropriate content, and are at the correct instructional level. Students can be encouraged to assist with this selection, for example, they could be given a choice of three texts to select;
- draw on their knowledge of the needs of the students to plan a prereading and several post-reading activities.

The activities may focus on learning goals related to figuring out words, learning vocabulary, developing fluency, or learning to use specific comprehension strategies. As they select activities, teachers typically ask themselves:

- How can these activities best meet the needs of my students?
- What are the potential challenges in this text that students will need support with and how can I do this?
- What prior knowledge of the text (structure, content, and language features) or topic will the students need to activate?
- What follow-up practice and support will the students require?
- Which activities are best used by students? How can I vary the activities so that some are for pairs, some are for the group, and some are for individual work?
- What will I need to explain or demonstrate so the students can use the activity independently or with peer support?

Planning also means organizing the resources necessary for the activities. This enables smooth transitions from one activity to another and minimizes time spent on management when the teacher is giving instruction to a group.

 For each group, the teacher can chart the texts and activities to be used over a one- or two-week period.

Bill made notes about a number of activities he might use as one group read an article about a mountaineer. He was not planning to use them all but wanted to have a variety ready depending on the needs that were revealed during instructional lessons and to allow extra choices for students who might complete the activity early.

Text title: Mountain Survivor

From Orbit Collections: *On the Edge*

Prereading activity	**Post-reading activity**
• Group discussion about what it means to be a professional mountaineer • Charting what students know about climbing in snow and ice • Discussion of what students know followed by identification of potential hazards • Introduction of key vocabulary – food drop, amputate, rations, frostbite, survival, overnight ascent • Students to make predictions based on key vocabulary	• Develop a glossary of key vocabulary from the text related to the theme of survival (to support vocabulary using development from text) • Chart to summarize key hazards to survival (to support summarization) • Discussion/explanation for an audience of what it must have been like for the mountaineers, providing evidence from the text to support their point of view (to support inference, links to prior knowledge, analysis)

from "Mountain Survivor" by Maggie Lilleby, *On the Edge*, Orbit Collections

There are many pre and post-reading activities that teachers can use to support metacognitive comprehension instruction. These may include independent activities, partner activities, group activities, or a combination of these. The critical aspect is that the teacher selects activities that will support student learning and development in reading comprehension. The following section provides examples of these activities.

Prereading activities

Prereading activities are designed to help prepare the students for their next instructional lesson. They will often be used to help students make connections with prior knowledge, for example, by giving them opportunities to brainstorm what they already know about a topic or to find out more about it. They can also be used to address potential challenges in the text, for example, by providing opportunities to explore the vocabulary associated with a topic or the features associated with a text type. The students bring the completed prereading activity to their next instructional lesson.

The teacher may start the activity with a brief explanation, but most activities should require minimal direction as long as the preparation has been thorough. The following examples show some ways of planning for high-quality, varied prereading activities.

Previewing a text

The students are preparing to read an informational text. The text relates to a theme they are studying in science. The teacher has identified a number of content and vocabulary challenges. In addition, the text structure uses subheadings and labeled diagrams. Students are asked to preview their copies of the text and to:

- predict what each section might be about and give reasons
- check key words in subheadings by using a glossary or other source to find clues as to what each section might be about
- record these clues for group discussion
- list questions they would like to explore when they read the text.

Preparing to read an argument

The students are preparing to read a persuasive text. This is the first example of the genre that the students have read in conjunction with a social studies topic. They are given the topic and asked to:

- list what they know about arguments in general
- think of two reasons for the argument and two reasons against it
- predict some of the vocabulary that the author might use.

Setting reading expectations for a report

The students are preparing to read a report of a cultural event. The teacher aims to support them with the content of the text and its structural features. The teacher provides each student with a copy of the text (or displays an enlarged version if it will be a shared reading lesson) and gives a short overview before asking the students to skim read the text and identify key words and phrases. Based on the overview and the key words found, the students are asked to predict what they expect the text to be about and list, draw, or make a diagram of what they already know about the event.

Overviewing a text

Key words

Key ideas

Complete the following statements:

When I overviewed the text, I found ...

I already know ...

I predict I will learn ...

Using graphic organizers to overview key words and ideas

The teacher asks the students to overview the text to determine what it will be about, what the main ideas will be, and what its purpose might be. They do this using a graphic organizer that the teacher has developed. The headings on the graphic organizer serve as "categories" for the students' overview. For example, to prepare for reading a nonfiction text with subheadings and tables, the teacher may list the subheadings and titles of the tables on the graphic organizer. As they skim the text, the students use the graphic organizer to record important key words and ideas from these sources. Illustrations and photographs are also considered as the students overview a text.

A variation uses a graphic organizer that gives prompts as well as spaces to record key words and ideas. The students note the key words and

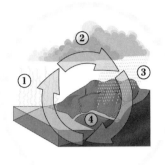

The Water Cycle from *Water in the Weather* by Pat Quinn, Skyrider* Double Takes

ideas and make predictions about the information they will find when they read the text later. They complete sentences to record their overview.

Using text features

The teacher wants to focus the students, attention on the structural features of the text. The students are told the structure of the text they will be reading, for example, a text that explains a process. They are given a copy of one or two diagrams from the text and are asked to use these to predict what the text will be about. The students explain what they already know about this topic.

Making connections with prior knowledge

Students make connections to their prior knowledge about a topic and use this knowledge to predict vocabulary.

- They list what they know about the theme or topic.
- They list what vocabulary they expect to find in the text.

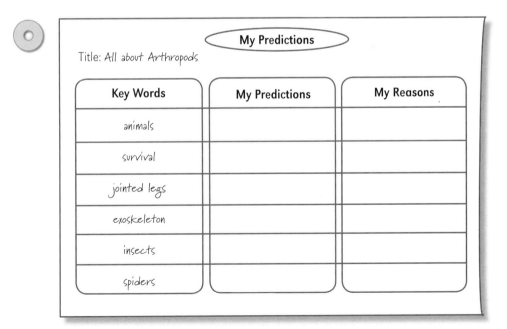

	My Predictions	
Title: All about Arthropods		
Key Words	**My Predictions**	**My Reasons**
animals		
survival		
jointed legs		
exoskeleton		
insects		
spiders		

Predicting from key words

The teacher provides the topic of the text for the next lesson and a list of key words from the text. The students use these words to predict what they will be reading about and give reasons to support their predictions.

Post-reading activities

At the time of preparation, the teacher carefully considers the activities that will build on the learning from the instructional lesson. These activities are selected in response to the learning goal and are based on students' needs.

Selecting post-reading activities

Post-reading activities can be used to:

- provide sustained practice of newly introduced comprehension strategies
- provide sustained opportunities to explore content and concepts introduced through the lesson
- maintain previously acquired skills, knowledge, and strategies
- prepare students for future reading or a rereading for a different purpose
- make links with content learning across the curriculum, for example, to a social studies topic or a science text
- encourage students to probe deeper into specific areas of comprehension
- establish routines and opportunities for independent, pair, and small-group learning.

The following examples demonstrate the variety of purposes and activities that can be used after an instructional reading comprehension lesson.

Practicing newly introduced comprehension strategies

A series of lessons have focused on developing student knowledge of text structure. Students have been reading reports (linked to their science topic and their writing instruction). The students now complete a graphic organizer that requires them to analyze the structure of a report by making notes about the information in each section.

Text Structure: Report

Title: Jamaica, My Home Country

Sections	This Tells Us About ...
Introduction	The person who is writing the report
Country file	Facts and figures about Jamaica
Land and climate	What the country looks like and gives information about the temperatures and rainfall through the year
People	Where the people of Jamaica came from, the languages they speak, and where they live
History	What happened to the indigenous people and how the Spanish and British ruled Jamaica until 1962

from "Jamaica: My Home Country" by Eugenie Brown,
A Sense of Place, Orbit Collections

Exploring content and concepts introduced through the lesson

The previous guided reading lesson focused on understanding the vocabulary that described an event in a narrative. As a follow-up, students complete an innovation on the text substituting synonyms for the original vocabulary. They do this activity in pairs. Once completed, they share their ideas with other group members, justifying their selections and giving one another constructive feedback.

The text says:

Wanted: Energetic babysitter for three calm children. Must love fast food and be good at basketball and soccer.

Innovation 1

Lively child minder for three serene children. Must adore takeout and be superb at basketball and soccer.

Innovation 2

Full-of-life caregiver for three quiet children. Must relish fast food and be talented at basketball and soccer.

from "Wanted" by Karen Anderson, *On the Job*, Orbit Collections

Maintaining previously acquired skills, knowledge, and strategies

Students have been learning strategies for figuring out words that they find difficult as they read. As a follow-up activity, students work in pairs. They each take turns at reading a section of the text they have previously read with the teacher. As they come to a word they are unsure of, they use the think-aloud approach to tell their partner which strategies would help them. The partner provides feedback before taking their turn.

Teresa and her partner are using the think-aloud approach to explain their strategies for figuring out unfamiliar words. Teresa writes "scorching" from the text onto a chart. As she thinks aloud, she erases and rewrites parts of the word as she explains to her partner.

> *I look through the word and think about the rest of the sentence.*
> *I think it's a verb because it was doing something to the writer's shoulders and it ends in -ing.*
> *I take off the -ing and look at what's left. I can see most of the word* score *inside.*
> *I replace the e with the ch sound – scorch – I put the -ing back on and say the whole word: it's scorching.*

Teresa's partner Jo, reads the sentence through aloud, and they discuss the word in context to confirm that "scorching" is correct.

See chapter 2 for more examples of strategies and activities for recognizing words.

Preparing for future reading

During the previous guided reading lesson, the group only completed half of a persuasive text. As a follow-up, the students were asked to predict three further arguments that the author may have included in the remainder of the text. Students were asked to give reasons for their predictions based on the content they had read so far.

Linking to cross-curricula learning content

The group has been reading a science text during instructional reading sessions. As a follow-up, each student keeps a glossary of the subject-specific vocabulary. They write a definition of each word based on context clues in the text, and where possible, draw a sketch that illustrates the word.

Probing deeper into specific areas of comprehension

Students have been learning about how to use the clues authors give them to help infer meaning. They have also been practicing writing sentences that infer information. In this activity, students read a section of text. They list the inferences they have made about the events and the characters. Each student gives the list to another student who identifies the clues that they think led to each inference.

Presenting a theme

Group lessons have provided instruction to assist students to comprehend a series of poems on a theme. The literary focus has been on imagery. The follow-up task is for the group to prepare a presentation of these poems to the rest of the class, highlighting how the author has used imagery for effect.

Summarizing

During the lesson, the students read a history text and were learning to use the comprehension strategy of summarizing. The learning goal was to identify key words in each paragraph, in particular subject-specific vocabulary and words that explain what, how, and why. The students were learning to use the key words to retell the most important ideas.

Following the lesson, the students used a list of key words (written onto a graphic organizer), then used the graphic organizer to verbally retell what they had read to a partner. The students then completed the graphic organizer using key words as prompts.

Summarizing		
Title: Into the Unknown		
Key Words: expedition explore trade routes discovery dangerous map adventure		
What happened?	**How did it happen?**	**Why did it happen?**
Lewis and Clark led an expedition to explore the western region of North America.	U.S. President Jefferson proposed it and chose Lewis to lead.	Jefferson wanted to know more about the region and to find trade routes.

from *Into the Unknown* by Jillian Sullivan, Skyrider* Investigations

Cloze

The teacher has prepared a cloze activity from a text the group has read. A typical cloze keeps the first sentence intact and then removes every seventh word. A cloze can be adapted for instructional purposes to suit the focus of the lesson (for example, a pronoun cloze would remove all pronouns; an adjective cloze would remove all adjectives). When making an instructional cloze activity:

- make sure there are sufficient clues in the text for each missing word
- select a variety of words according to the purpose (for example, descriptive words can include verbs and adverbs as well as adjectives)
- choose at least one word that is important for cohesion (for example, *thus, consequently*)
- try to select some words that have several possibilities as this will lead to discussion and further vocabulary development.

Students complete the cloze either independently or with a partner. They then share their responses and justify their selection of vocabulary. It is important that the teacher and students mark the cloze together. Cooperative marking (students self-marking during a discussion with the teacher) allows high-quality discussion on why a word was correctly placed and the strategies students used to select the correct word. Teaching can draw attention to clues in the text. Teachers can encourage students to justify why a word was chosen and to evaluate and give feedback on the selections made by their peers.

Character web

Based on a story that has been read in the lesson, the teacher writes the name of a character in the middle of the web. The students brainstorm associations and make connections between ideas. They discuss the connections with one another and the significance of the connections to the development of the main ideas or the plot.

Venn diagram

The students use a Venn diagram to help them organize their thinking about the text. They can use this to compare it with another text, or to compare two characters. They write the differences on opposite sides and the similarities in the middle.

Table of contents

The group has been learning to identify the most important points in a text. This activity requires each student to use these points to write a table of contents. Students could also be asked to provide a brief overview for each heading.

Systems, routines, and resources for reading activities

Teachers use a variety of systems for managing reading activities and resources. The aim is to keep disruption to a minimum during instructional time while ensuring that every student who is not with the teacher is engaged in a focused reading activity. Time spent at the start of the school year to prepare resources, to show the students how the systems work, and to practice starting and changing activities will save much time later. Teachers can establish routines for what to do when an activity is completed, where to find materials, and when and how to seek help.

Organizational systems

Two commonly used systems for the management of reading activities are reading group boxes and reading task boards.

Reading group boxes

In this system, the teacher sets up a box for each reading group where all reading comprehension resources and materials for the week are stored. The names of the students in each group are written on the outside of the box. These need to be able to be changed as groups change. Each group box is usually a different color.

The box is refilled each week with copies of the texts the students will be reading and copies of the prereading and post-reading activities. The students' reading notebooks can be stored in the box if the students are to use them as they work. The boxes can be stored on a bookshelf or on the group's table. Group members access the materials as required. When a group is working with the teacher, the group box goes with them. The teacher (or the students) may assign one person to take responsibility for keeping the materials in order through the week.

Reading Organization

Group				
A	With the Teacher	Graphic Organizer A	Partner Reading (expected)	Response Task A
B	Independent Research	With the Teacher	Partner Reading (new text)	Response Task D
C	Vocabulary Task A	Response Task C	With the Teacher	Vocabulary Task B
D	Group Meeting	Graphic Organizer B		With the Teacher

Reading task boards

A reading task board is a large chart. The reading groups are listed down one side. Across from each group are spaces for the names of reading activities. These may be written on sticky notes, or the teacher can use magnets (on a magnetic board), pockets (on a pocket chart), or sticky dots so that they can be moved. The students find their group name and see which activities they are to do for the day, completing the activities in the order they are placed.

This is an effective way of developing reading group routines, but all the activities must be prepared ahead of time. Activities and related materials need to be stored in one or more containers. Teachers label the activities as they prepare them so that students can identify them quickly. Activities that are not being used should be stored separately. The teacher updates the task board each day to ensure a rotation of instructional time and prereading and post-reading activities.

Graphic organizers

Teachers in grades 3 to 8 regularly use graphic organizers to scaffold student learning. Graphic organizers are tools for organizing information and are frequently used for prereading and post-reading activities. They may also be used during reading as the teacher and students work through text. It is important that students understand the generic (rather than activity-specific) nature of graphic organizers and that teachers give clear instructions for their use.

A variety of templates can be found on the Internet and in teacher resource books, as well as the collections that most teachers share in the course of their work. Teachers can also design their own graphic organizers for specific learning goals, remembering that they should remain generic, not specific to one text or activity. The most useful graphic organizers are those that can be applied in a variety of lessons with a variety of texts: Venn diagrams are an excellent example of a generic graphic organizer.

The following are four examples of graphic organizers that can be used for a variety of purposes.

Venn diagram

Purpose – to explore relationships between ideas in text or between texts

Before reading – use to organize ideas based on previous reading and experience

During reading – add to the diagram as text unfolds and relationships (for example, between ideas, characters, cause and effect) become evident

After reading – use to clarify and summarize relationships.

Exploring the setting

Purpose – to explore the setting of a narrative text by identifying where the text takes place, what the place is like, and significant features of the setting

Before reading – based on an initial introduction of the setting, students predict what the setting might be like and how it might contribute to the story (can also be used to activate their prior knowledge and to identify their familiarity with the setting)

After reading – use to summarize the effects of the setting on the narrative and to focus on knowledge of text structure.

Two alternatives are given to enable flexible use: teachers can adapt these to suit specific purposes. These graphic organizers can also be expanded to ask students to note an alternative setting, explaining and giving reasons for their choices. This could include how the alternative setting would fit with the current story structure.

Plot sequence

Purpose – to identify features of narrative text and to focus on the development of plot (and subplot)

After reading – to record features of the plot and subplot development
Remind students that a narrative may have more than one plot.

Features of plot development could include the rising action, parallel storylines, flashbacks, or the retelling of an incident from another character's point of view. The graphic organizer can be modified to focus on different features of plot development.

Problems and solutions

Purpose – to identify the problems and solutions within the plot
After reading – to record the problems and solutions, indicating the settings and characters involved with each problem.

The components of a metacognitive comprehension instruction program

The following section looks at putting together the components of a metacognitive comprehension instruction program. It provides three examples of classroom timetables for the reading block that exemplify what metacognitive comprehension instruction might look like over a six to eight week period. In each example, the class has been organized into four ability groups but this can be modified. Together, the examples illustrate the variety of ways that teachers can plan and manage their reading comprehension program based on the following key understandings:

- Teachers use information about their students' needs to organize their reading comprehension programs.
- Programs vary and change through the year.
- Programs are usually developed for a six to eight week block during which time teachers modify the program to meet the changing needs of their students.
- Teachers consider the needs of their students when determining the reading comprehension activities, both for instruction with the teacher and for independent group activities.
- Teachers consider the needs of the students and the kind of text to determine the most appropriate teaching approaches, for example, shared, guided, or reciprocal reading.

The examples show either shared, guided, or reciprocal reading used as the main approach, but this can be varied with teachers selecting the approach that best suits their students' needs and the challenges of the text. The supporting approaches described in chapter 6 can also be used.

Each example is based on a fifty to sixty minute reading block. It does not include reading aloud to students, which usually takes place outside of this session. The time is divided into two twenty-minute instructional lessons with two groups per day, allowing extra time to check on the progress of other groups and for transitions. This timing is not inflexible: teachers will frequently adapt their time according to the situation and the needs of the students. Following one group across an organizational chart shows the cycle of prereading activity, lesson with the teacher, and post-reading activity. There may be more than one activity either side of the instructional lesson.

The examples given here are exactly that: examples. Teachers will devise a program that suits the demands of their school or district, the needs of their students, and their own ability to manage group-based teaching. Some teachers may wish to start with two or three larger groups and add more groups when their routines are in place. These examples can be used as models to work toward.

Classroom timetable examples

1. Organization chart (shared reading)

	Day 1	Day 2	Day 3	Day 4
Group 1	**Shared reading** Repeated reading Vocabulary sorting	Text structure Prior knowledge: structure	**Shared reading** Repeated reading Vocabulary sorting	Text structure Prior knowledge: structure
Group 2	Prior knowledge: structure **Shared reading**	Repeated reading Vocabulary sorting Text structure	Prior knowledge: structure **Shared reading**	Repeated reading Vocabulary sorting Text structure
Group 3	Text structure Prior knowledge: structure	**Shared reading** Repeated reading Vocabulary sorting	Text structure Prior knowledge: structure	**Shared reading** Repeated reading Vocabulary sorting
Group 4	Repeated reading Vocabulary sorting Text structure	Prior knowledge: structure **Shared reading**	Repeated reading Vocabulary sorting	Prior knowledge: structure **Shared reading**

This example uses **shared reading** as the main instructional approach (see chapter 6). Each group has a different text, selected to ensure a match between student needs and reading levels and between the text content and structure. The activities are designed to be common to all groups but the level of support required and the level of achievement will vary according to the abilities of the group.

Group activities for this example include:

a. prior knowledge activity to prepare students for the structure of the text
b. follow-up activity that requires the students to read the text again (repeated reading)
c. vocabulary sorting activity
d. text structure activity that uses a graphic organizer that students complete to demonstrate their understanding.

Activating prior knowledge

The prereading activity focuses the students' attention on the structural features of the nonfiction text and how knowledge of text features can support comprehension. Students are told the structure and topic of the text and are given a copy of several illustrations from the text. They are asked to use these to predict what the text will be about and to explain what they already know about the topic.

Repeated reading

This may be done independently or with a partner. If it is done with a partner, teachers can ask students to focus on particular aspects of fluency and accuracy or on comprehension strategies they are practicing and provide each other with feedback (see chapters 4 and 5). It also provides another opportunity to consolidate new vocabulary, especially subject-specific or technical vocabulary.

Vocabulary sorting activity

The teacher provides a list of words from the text. These words can be sorted into a variety of categories. Examples include, words that stand for something you can touch, see, hear, taste, or smell; words that stand for something you can do or be; or words that stand for something found inside, outside, at school, at home, at a workplace, or in the community.

Text structure graphic organizer

Different texts have different features. This activity draws the students' attention to these features and how they influence comprehension. For example, an explanation will say how and why things work. There will be an introductory statement of definition, reasons to explain why or how, and a summary. Nouns, pronouns, signal words (*because*, *if*, *then*), and linking words (*first*, *next*, *finally*) will be prevalent. A graphic organizer will require students to find this information.

2. Organization chart (guided reading)

	Day 1	Day 2	Day 3	Day 4
Group 1	Prior knowledge activity **Guided reading**	Interactive cloze, innovating on text Vocabulary activities	Prior knowledge activity **Guided reading**	Interactive cloze, innovating on text Vocabulary activities
Group 2	**Guided reading** Vocabulary activities	Interactive cloze, innovating on text Prior knowledge activity	**Guided reading** Vocabulary activities	Interactive cloze, innovating on text Prior knowledge activity
Group 3	Vocabulary activities Interactive cloze, innovating on text	Prior knowledge activity **Guided reading**	Vocabulary activities Interactive cloze, innovating on text	Prior knowledge activity **Guided reading**
Group 4	Interactive cloze, innovating on text Prior knowledge activity	**Guided reading** Vocabulary activities	Interactive cloze, innovating on text Prior knowledge	**Guided reading** Vocabulary activities

This example uses **guided reading** as the main instructional approach (see chapter 6). Each group has a text that is specific to their reading level and has a match between student need and text content. The activities are designed to be common to all groups, but the level of support required and the level of achievement will vary.

Group activities for this example include:

a. prior knowledge prereading activity to prepare students for the text

b. post-reading activity that requires the students to complete an interactive cloze activity or innovation based on the text

c. post-reading vocabulary activities to embed the vocabulary students encountered during instruction.

Activating prior knowledge

In the first four weeks of the program, the teacher provides a preview of each text and a list of some of the vocabulary. Based on the preview and the key words, students are asked to predict what they expect the text to be about, list what they already know about this, and identify any questions they have about it. In the second four weeks, the teacher will have the students preview the text using a graphic organizer where they add their own key ideas and vocabulary.

Interactive cloze

This activity provides learning opportunities about grammar, vocabulary, and structure and how these affect content and meaning. The teacher has taught the students how to complete a cloze activity before it has become a group activity. The cloze is made from sections of the text the students have read during the guided reading lesson. Students complete the cloze either independently or with a partner. The group then meets to share, justify, and discuss their vocabulary choices. The cloze is reviewed with the teacher, who may either lead the review through questioning or observe as the students take responsibility for the discussion (peer assessment). Students offer their responses and justify them, making group decisions about which words are best for each gap. *(See also Peer and self-assessment on page 21 in chapter 1.)*

The focus of discussion around marking will be on the strategies that the students used and the decisions they made to determine their choices. Finally, the students read the instructional text again to check against their choices and to focus on repeated reading.

Innovating on a text

See the activity on page 266 above.

Vocabulary activities

Two vocabulary activities are organized to embed new learning. These are for use after reading. Students complete both activities for each word under study. The words will be selected from the different vocabulary encountered during the guided reading lesson. For example:

A synonym wheel – using target words (for example, exemplify), the students find words that mean the same and related phrases.

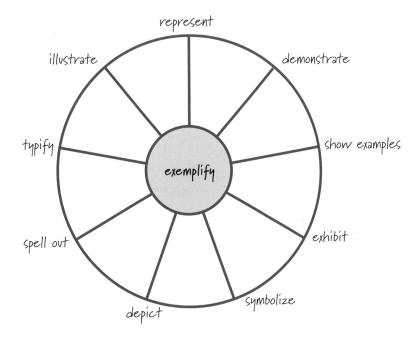

A classification activity – the students sort words according to how they relate to their lives. For example, they sort words based on how they fit into their experience, describe someone they know, describe an event they have experienced, describe a feeling they have felt, or relate to something they have seen others do.

3. Organization chart (reciprocal reading)

	Day 1	Day 2	Day 3	Day 4
Group 1	**Reciprocal reading** L of KWL Strategy activity	Vocabulary Flowchart Prereading: KWV	**Reciprocal reading** L of KWL Strategy activity	Vocabulary Flowchart Prereading KWV activity
Group 2	Prereading: KWV **Reciprocal reading**	L of KWL Strategy activity	Prereading: KWV **Reciprocal reading**	L of KWL Strategy activity Vocabulary Flowchart
Group 3	Vocabulary Flowchart KWV	**Reciprocal reading** L of KWL Vocabulary	Vocabulary Flowchart Prereading: KWV	**Reciprocal reading** L of KWL Strategy activity
Group 4	L of KWL Strategy activity Vocabulary Flowchart	Prereading: KWV **Reciprocal reading**	L of KWL Strategy activity Vocabulary Flowchart	Prereading: KWV **Reciprocal reading**

This example uses **reciprocal reading** as the main instructional approach (see chapter 6). Each group has a different nonfiction text, selected to ensure a match between student needs and reading levels and between text content and structure. The activities are designed to be common to all groups, but the level of support required and the level of achievement will vary.

Group activities for this example include:

a. prior knowledge activity (adapting the KWL activity) to prepare students for the text

b. follow-up activity that requires the students to identify what they have learned from reading and to compare this with what they knew prior to reading

c. vocabulary definition activity

d. comprehension strategy activity.

Activating prior knowledge

The prereading activity KWL (Ogle, 1986) requires students to list what they already know, what they would like to find out, and what they have learned. In this example, KWL has been adapted to use a vocabulary focus so that students list what they know, what they would like to find out, and what vocabulary they expect to encounter. This is referred to in the chart as KWV.

Reflecting on learning

This activity uses the L (what we learn) of the KWL. It is completed as a post-reading activity.

Vocabulary activity

This activity focuses on giving definitions of new words from their context. Students work in pairs from a list of words compiled over the course of the lesson. They take turns at giving accurate definitions for these words. They then return to the text to check that the definition is correct in the context. The teacher can also use any other appropriate vocabulary activity if different needs arise during the lesson (see chapter 3).

A comprehension strategy activity

A post-reading activity will provide additional practice with the comprehension strategy that was focused on during the lesson. (This may also occur where there are two or more strategies being explored.) For example, a flowchart graphic organizer may be used for students to record their summaries of events in a recount or explanation. As a further example, the students may be asked to practice what they are learning about self-questioning to help them comprehend text. Each student formulates questions about the text (including literal, investigative, and evaluative questions). These are then presented to other group members as a quiz. See chapter 5 for further examples of activities for comprehension strategies.

Summary

Group instruction is effective for both the teacher and the students when students of similar ability are grouped together, when reading activities are organized ahead of time, and when systems and routines are well established. Ensuring that all students are comfortable with the group reading routines and that they all understand the expectations on them are necessary for groups to function effectively.

There are many possible combinations of approaches and activities when forming a metacognitive comprehension instruction program. This chapter has focused on three of these possibilities. The most important aspects of working with groups are the deliberate choices that teachers make about organization, content, approaches, and activities based on the information they have about the needs of their students. As students' needs change, so too will the mix of teaching approaches and activities to develop and extend the students' comprehension learning. As teachers become more experienced in identifying the needs of their students and in adjusting their instructional choices, they learn to develop a rich and dynamic approach to comprehension instruction that promotes metacognitive learners and that is constantly informed by evidence.

References and recommended reading

Block, C. C. and Pressley, M. (2001). *Comprehension Instruction: Research-based Best Practices*. New York, New York: The Guilford Press.

Daniels, H. (1994). *Literature Circles: Voice and Choice in the Student-Centered Classroom*. York, Maine: Stenhouse.

Dowhower, S. L. (1999). "Supporting a Strategic Stance in the Classroom: A Comprehension Framework for Helping Teachers Help Students to Be Strategic". *The Reading Teacher*, 52(7), pp. 672–683.

Fountas, I. and Pinnell, G. S. (2001). *Guiding Readers and Writers (Grades 3–6): Teaching Comprehension, Genre, and Content Literacy*. Portsmouth, New Hampshire: Heinemann.

Ministry of Education (2006). *Effective Literacy Practice in Years 5 to 8*. Wellington, New Zealand: Learning Media.

Ogle, D. E. (1986) "K-W-L: A Teaching Model That Develops Active Reading of Expository Text". *The Reading Teacher*, 39 (6). pp. 564–570.

Palinscar A. S. and Brown, A. L. (1984). "Reciprocal Teaching of Comprehension-fostering and Comprehension-monitoring Activities". *Cognition and Instruction*, 1, pp.117–175.

Rog, L. J. (2003). *Guided Reading Basics: Organizing, Managing, and Implementing a Balanced Literacy Program in K–3*. Portland, Maine: Stenhouse.

Trehearne, Miriam (2005). *Nelson Language Arts Grades 3–6 Teacher's Resource Book*. Toronto: Nelson, a division of Thomson Canada Limited.

Valencia, S. W. and Buly, M. R. (2004). "Behind Test Scores: What Struggling Readers Really Need". *The Reading Teacher*, 57(6), pp. 520–531.

Vygotsky, L. S. (1978). *Mind in Society: The Development of Higher Psychological Processes*. Cambridge, Massachusetts: Harvard University Press.

Glossary

affix: a word part that can be added (fixed) to the beginning or end of a base or root word to alter its meaning

analogy: a comparison between similar things, used to make them easier to understand

anecdotal record: informal, dated notes made to describe observed behavior

antonym: a word opposite in meaning to another

automaticity: the fluent processing of information that requires little effort or attention

blends: see consonant blends

collaboration: two or more people working together to achieve a common goal

consonant blends: two or more consonants that appear together in a word, with each consonant retaining its own sound

decoding: analyzing spoken or graphic symbols of a familiar language to determine their intended meaning

derivations: words that have been formed by adding affixes to an existing root or base word; words that have their origins in other languages

genre: a category used to classify literary works, usually by form, technique, or content

incidental learning: unplanned or unintentional learning that results from other activities

instructional strategies: the deliberate acts of teaching that are used to achieve a particular purpose

intonation: the way a speaker's voice rises and falls to express the meanings of spoken phrases and sentences

language-rich environment: an environment in which there is a wide and varied use of written, oral, and visual language

mental modeling: demonstrating how to perform a task or use a strategy in which the learner copies the expert to learn the modeled strategy or skill

metacognitive: a term that describes the processes that learners use to think and talk about their thinking, articulating what they know, what they can do, and how they can apply their learning in new contexts

metacognitive awareness: the active application of metacognition (see above)

mind map: a graphic representation of oral or written information

morphemic analysis: strategy in which the meanings of words are determined or inferred by examining their structure and parts

onset and rime: the initial letters (onset) and the following vowel and consonants (rime) in a syllable

orthographic knowledge: knowledge of how the sounds in words are written

pace: the speed at which one reads a text to convey or uncover the author's intended meaning

phoneme: the smallest segment of sound in spoken language, for example, a, ch, k

phonemic awareness: the ability to hear, identify, and manipulate the individual sounds in spoken words

phonics: a way of teaching reading, writing, and spelling that emphasizes basic symbol–sound relationships

phonological awareness: a term that includes phonemic awareness of individual sounds as well as listening to sounds

prefix: a part of a word that is attached to the beginning of words to modify their meaning

prosody: a term used to refer to the pitch, loudness, tempo, and rhythm patterns of spoken language

recursive: repeating itself

root words: (also referred to as base words) the basic part of a word that carries the main meaning

scaffold: guidance and support that is provided as students gradually take responsibility for their learning

scaffolded practice: a practice in which guidance and support are available as needed with the ultimate aim for students to take responsibility for their learning

success criteria: the measures or levels of performance that will count as success toward achieving a goal

syllabification: forming or dividing words into syllables

syllable: a unit of language that consists of or represents one vowel sound and forms the whole or part of a word

synonym: a word or phrase similar in meaning to another

syntactic knowledge: knowledge of the grammatical rules of language

text: a piece of spoken, written, or visual communication

two-way feedback: the provision of feedback between two or more people

verb tenses: verbs used to express time (past, present, or future)

vocabulary: all the words of a language that are used and understood by a particular person or group

word recognition: the process of determining the pronunciation and meaning of a spoken and written word

References to Student Materials

Anderson, Karen (2001). "Wanted". Orbit Collections *On the Job*. Wellington: Learning Media Limited.

Bilbrough, Norman(2005). "The Wave". Power Zone* *Adrenalin*. Toronto: Nelson, a division of Thomson Canada Limited.

Bishop, Nic (2000). *The Living Rain Forest*. Skyrider* Chapter Books Grade 4. Wellington: Learning Media Limited.

Bonallack, John (2005). "Sleep-Who Needs It?" Power Zone* *Sleep*. Toronto: Nelson, a division of Thomson Canada Limited.

Bonallack, John (2007). *Switched On*. Skyrider* Investigations Grade 6. Toronto: Nelson, a division of Thomson Canada Limited.

Brown, Eugenie (2004). "Jamaica: My Home Country". Orbit Collections *A Sense of Place*. Wellington: Learning Media Limited.

Frances, Helen (2005). *Blubber and Blowholes*. Write Tools Grade 4. Wellington: Learning Media Limited.

Gaynor, Bill (2006). *Tsunami*. Skyrider* Double Takes Grade 6. Toronto: Nelson, a division of Thomson Canada Limited.

Green, Rebecca (2005). "Making A Difference". Power Zone* *Leaving Your Mark*. Toronto: Nelson, a division of Thomson Canada Limited.

Green, Rebecca (2005). *Blackout*. Skyrider* Investigations Grade 6. Toronto: Nelson, a division of Thomson Canada Limited.

Haakanson, Sven (2004). *Living with the Nenets*. Skyrider* Double Takes Grade 5. Toronto: Nelson, a division of Thomson Canada Limited.

Hager, Mandy (2002). "The Curious Case of the Midnight Muncher". Orbit Collections *A Mystery to Me*. Wellington: Learning Media Limited.

Hager, Mandy (2006). *Energy of the Future*. Skyrider* Double Takes Grade 6. Toronto: Nelson, a division of Thomson Canada Limited.

Hesse, Karen (1998). *Just Juice*. New York: Scholastic Inc.

Hiatt Harlow, Joan (2001). *Joshua's Song*. New York: Aladdin Paperbacks.

Lilleby, Maggie (2004). "Mountain Survivor". Orbit Collections *On the Edge*. Wellington: Learning Media Limited.

Mackenzie, Anna (2004). "Strangers in the Landscape". Orbit Collections *On the Edge*. Wellington: Learning Media Limited.

Marriott, Janice (2000). *The Refugees*. Skyrider* Chapter Books Grade 6. Wellington: Learning Media Limited.

Morris, Rod (2001). *Baby Dragons*. Skyrider* Shared Reading nonfiction Set B. Wellington: Learning Media Limited.

Paris, Susan (2004). *Hiyomi and the Moon Men*. Skyrider* Investigations Grade 4. Toronto: Nelson, a division of Thomson Canada Limited.

Paris, Susan (2006). *Pioneer Days*. Skyrider* Investigations Grade 5. Toronto: Nelson, a division of Thomson Canada Limited.

Quinn, Pat (1999). *Sky Moves*. Skyrider* Shared Reading nonfiction Set C. Wellington: Learning Media Limited.

Quinn, Pat (2002). *Water in the Weather*. Skyrider* Double Takes Grade 3. Toronto: Nelson, a division of Thomson Canada Limited.

Sullivan, Jillian (2005). *Into the Unknown*. Toronto: Nelson, a division of Thomson Canada Limited.

Taylor, William (1999). *Harry Houdini – Wonderdog!* Skyrider* Chapter Books Grade 5. Wellington: Learning Media Limited.

Tu`akoi, Feana (2005). "Eating Snow". Power Zone* *Lost? Found!* Toronto: Nelson, a division of Thomson Canada Limited.

Young, Ashleigh (2006). *Wild Ideas*. Skyrider* Shared Reading fiction Set D. Wellington: Learning Media Limited.

Young, Ashleigh (2007). *Takeoff!*. Skyrider* Investigations Grade 6. Toronto: Nelson, a division of Thomson Canada Limited.

In the United States of America, the Skyrider titles appear under the Orbit brand and the Power Zone titles appear under the High Wire brand.

Index